ST. ANNE

Grandmother of Our Saviour

The Holy Family. El Greco.

St. Anne

GRANDMOTHER OF OUR SAVIOUR

BY

Frances Parkinson Keyes

HAWTHORN BOOKS, INC., *Publishers*, NEW YORK

Nihil Obstat

John J. Foley

CENSOR DEPUTATUS

Imprimatur

✠ Matthew F. Brady

BISHOP of Manchester

Manchester, September 29, 1955

The Nihil obstat and imprimatur are official dec-
larations that a book or pamphlet is free of doctrinal
or moral error. No implication is contained therein
that those who have granted the nihil obstat and
imprimatur agree with the contents, opinions or
statements expressed.

Endpaper: *Presentation of the Virgin in Temple. Titian.*
Royal Academy, Venice.

Back of jacket: *Virgin and Child with St. Anne.*
Leonardo and pupils. Louvre, Paris.

To my ten grandchildren

PETER BOWEN KEYES

MARGARETTA MAIN KEYES

JOHN PARKINSON KEYES II

FRANCES PARKINSON KEYES II

SARAH LOUISE KEYES

CATHERINE MACARTHUR KEYES

DAVID JOHNSON KEYES

VIRGINIA BOWEN KEYES

LOUISE KEYES

FRANCES KEYES

With their grandmother's love and the hope that the blessing of
St. Anne, Grandmother of Our Saviour,
Will always rest upon them.

I do not know it, but I believe it because I feel it.

ANON.

By Frances Parkinson Keyes

FICTION

The Royal Box
Steamboat Gothic
Joy Street
Dinner at Antoine's
Came A Cavalier
The River Road
Also the Hills
Crescent Carnival
All That Glitters
Fielding's Folly
The Great Tradition
Parts Unknown
Honor Bright
The Safe Bridge
Senator Marlowe's Daughter
Lady Blanche Farm
Queen Anne's Lace
The Career of David Noble
The Old Gray Homestead

NON-FICTION

The Frances Parkinson Keyes
    Cookbook
The Cost of a Best Seller
All This Is Louisiana
Capital Kaleidoscope
Silver Seas and Golden Cities
Letters from a Senator's Wife

POETRY

The Happy Wanderer

JUVENILE

Once on Esplanade

CATHOLIC INTEREST

St. Anne: Grandmother of Our
    Saviour
Therese: Saint of A Little Way
The Grace of Guadulupe
Bernadette of Lourdes
Along A Little Way

Frances Parkinson Keyes' Books

have also been published in: England, Germany, Finland, Spain, Denmark, Sweden, France, Italy, Norway, Holland, Japan, Czechoslovakia, Argentina, Mexico, Brazil and Switzerland.

Contents

INTRODUCTION: Our Lord had a Grandmother, too   15

PART I: The Life of St. Anne   31

PART II: Cult of St. Anne   115

PART III: Songs, Poems and Canticles of St. Anne   157

APPENDIX: References, Bibliography, Author's Note   175

List of Illustrations

~~~~

The Holy Family. El Greco.   *Frontispiece*

                                                                  Page

The Holy Family. Bernardino Luini.   14
Miraculous statue of St. Anne. Convent of Santa Ana, Avila.   21
The Holy Family. Dominican Convent, Madrigal.   22
Polychromed wooden figure of St. Anne.   24
Marker at St. Anne's Shrine, Isle La Motte, Vermont.   25
Shrine of St. Anne, Milford, Vermont.   26
St. Anne with the Virgin. Benzoni.   27
Medallion of St. Anne with the Virgin in vegetable ivory. From
 Arequipa, Peru.   28
Tree of Jesse. Tapestry, Reims Cathedral.   30
St. Anne. Royal Library, Windsor Castle.   38
Parents of St. Anne. C. von Coninxloo.   41
Story of St. Joachim and St. Anne. Gaudenzio Ferrari.   48
The Meeting of St. Anne and St. Joachim at the Golden Gate.
 Master of Moulins.   50
Nativity of Mary. Church of St. Séverin, Paris.   54
The Birth of the Virgin. Anonymous, 16th Century.   55
Nativity of the Virgin. After Murillo.   56
St. Anne Teaching the Virgin. Pinturicchio.   63
Presentation at the Temple. F. Fiori detto il Baroccio.   64
Presentation of the Virgin at the Temple. Church of St. Séverin,
 Paris.   66
Presentation at the Temple. Andrea Oroagna.   67
St. Anne Teaching the Virgin. Murillo.   68
St. Anne Teaching the Virgin. School of Murillo.   70
Central panel of triptich of carved, painted and gilded wood.
 Die Heilige Sippe. Franconian, circa 1500.   72
St. Anne Teaching the Virgin. Porcelain tile.   77
The Virgin and St. Anne. Lorenzo da Sanseverino.   78

The Betrothal of the Virgin. Church of St. Séverin, Paris.   82

The Betrothal of the Virgin. Wood carving.   83

The Annunciation. Bronzino.   84

Altarpiece from the Church of St. Anne in Granada, showing St. Anne and St. Joachim in adoration of the Virgin.   86

The Flight into Egypt. Church of St. Séverin, Paris.   90

Virgin and Child with St. Anne. Leonardo and pupils.   91

Madonna and Child with St. Anne. Bernardino Luini.   92

St. Anne with the Child Jesus. Convent entrance, Malaga.   94

The Death of St. Anne. Quentin Matsys.   97

The Glorification of St. Anne. J. B. Francken.   100

Ceiling of the interior crypt, Cathedral of St. Anne, Apt.   103

Reliquary of St. Anne, St. Anne's Cathedral, Apt.   111

St. Anne and the Virgin, gilded wood statue in the Cathedral at Vence, in Provence, not far from Apt.   112

The Madonna and Child, St. Anne and Mary, St. Elizabeth and St. John. Church of Santa Maria Antigua, Rome.   114

Flower mosaic. St. Ann's Well, Buxton.   120

Flower mosaic. St. Ann's Well, Buxton.   121

Votive Offering from the St. Anne. Rear wall, Memorial Chapel, Ste. Anne de Beaupré.   122

St. Joachim presenting the Virgin at the Temple. Brother Luke Recollect. Side altar, Memorial Chapel, Ste. Anne de Beaupré.   124

St. Anne presenting the Virgin at the Temple. Brother Luke Recollect. Side altar, Memorial Chapel, Ste. Anne de Beaupré.   125

Miraculous painting. Attributed to LeBrun. Main altar, Memorial Chapel, Ste. Anne de Beaupré.   126

Miraculous Statue, Ste. Anne de Beaupré.   129

Statue of Ste. Anne d'Auray.   130

Figurine of St. Anne and the Virgin. Quimper pottery.   136

Procession leaving St. Anne's Church, New Orleans, on her feast day.   142

South portal of the Monastery, Daphni.   148

The Birth of the Virgin. Mosaic at the Monastery, Daphni.   151

The Promise of a Child to St. Anne and St. Joachim. Mosaic at the Monastery, Daphni.   152

The Presentation at the Temple. Mosaic at the Monastery, Daphni.   153

Statue of St. Anne holding the Virgin and the Virgin holding the Christ Child. Cathedral, Avila.   156

The Virgin with Her Son and St. Anne. Masaccio.   171

Introduction

The Holy Family. Bernardino Luini.

Introduction

Our Lord Had a Grandmother, Too

"St. Anne, Grandmother of Our Saviour, pray for us."

This is the way the beautiful litany to St. Anne begins. It continues by designating her as "Mother of Mary, the Blessed Virgin and Mother" —"Ark of the Covenant"—"Root of Jesse"—"Fruitful Vine"—"Daughter of the Patriarchs"—"Consolation of the Afflicted" and in many other ways, all of which have their appropriate symbolism. But it is significant that she is hailed and petitioned as the grandmother of Jesus Christ, even before she is hailed and petitioned as the mother of the Holy Virgin.

There are several reasons for this. One is that, from the emotional viewpoint of most human beings, she seems closer to Christ than any other saint and closer to us even than the Blessed Mother.[1] For she, too, was a human being, conceived and born, living and dying, like any other; and also, like any other, conceiving herself as the result of natural union with her husband; yet our Divine Saviour was flesh of her flesh and bone of her bone. Of course, in one sense, Mary was a human being, too; but her Immaculate Conception, her virgin motherhood and her glorious Assumption set her apart from other human beings, whereas there is nothing about St. Anne that does. It is through this shared humanity that she brings them so close to Christ. Even her mortal remains are the relics nearest to Our Saviour, since, because of the Ascension and Assumption, we have none either of Him or of His mother.

Another aspect of the emotional viewpoint which brings St. Anne

· 15 ·

close to human beings lies in the fact that she achieved her honored place in the Calendar of Saints without suffering martyrdom or even because of withdrawing from the world after taking perpetual vows of poverty, chastity and obedience and leading a life of penance and privation. Her father and her husband were both men of substantial means and lofty character; she was sheltered and cherished always. She lived the normal life of a daughter, wife, mother and grandmother, under conditions which were, for the most part, favorable to happiness, comfort and general well being. But these did not prevent her from the fervent practice of her faith or from a true realization of the comparative value between earthly benefits and heavenly rewards. St. James was later to declare, "Religion clean and undefiled before God and the Father is this: to visit the fatherless and widows in their tribulation and to keep oneself unspotted from this world." Anne was charitable to all and her own life was one of purity and consecration; but she managed to do all that she did and be all that she was while still surrounded by her family and occupied by the manifold cares of her household. This is an ideal toward which many a woman, who shrinks from the thought of martyrdom and who has no vocation for a cloistered life, feels that she may strive. It is—she hopes and believes—not beyond her powers to attempt, with God's help. Just as Thérèse, the gentle young saint of Lisieux, helped many simple souls to find "A Little Way" to salvation when a greater way would have been beyond their capabilities, so St. Anne, through the sanctification of her normal life reveals that similar sanctification may always be possible in other everyday lives.

Still another reason for making St. Anne's position pre-eminent is that she was, so to speak, "the bridge between the Old Law and the New Testament." That is the way Roger Baudier, one of the most eminent American writers of our day, on both religious and historic subjects, has described her, and I cannot think of any more graphic and convincing manner. "Mary gave the world the Saviour," Baudier goes on to explain, "St. Anne gave the world that Mary, her daughter. St. Anne, as it were, closed the Old Testament and brought to the world the beginning of a new order. She played a definite part in God's plan for the salvation of mankind. Since then, redemption of the world was such a stupendous deed, and meant so much to the world, St. Anne partakes of the glory of it, and deservedly holds a high place in our esteem. If God did so much to honor His creature, Anne, the wife of Joachim, to be the grandmother of His Son, should we not honor her, too?"

All this now seems to me entirely logical and fitting; but I confess that this did not happen until long after I had written the greeting on one of the Christmas cards, which I prepare every year and send out to my personal friends and professional associates. On this occasion the title of the greeting was "Our Lord Had a Grandmother, Too," and I cannot even take credit for that. It was my secretary, Deanie Bullock, who suggested it after I had finished reading her the script and then turned to her, saying, "Can you think of a good title for that?"

I believe it was partly because the title Deanie suggested was so significant and the format of the card—illustrated by Bernardino Luini's sketch for his painting of the Holy Family—was so attractive that the greeting itself met with such an overwhelming response. At all events, friends of friends began to ask if I had a copy left over that I could spare; and early in the new year, Katharine McKiever, who is on the editorial staff of the N.C.W.C. News Service in Washington, and Muna Lee, an adviser in the Bureau of Inter-American Affairs in the State Department, both asked me if I would not make such slight deletions, additions and revisions in the text as would render a personal message suitable to use in article form. Astonished, but gratified—indeed, deeply moved—by their request, I complied with it; and the result was published, in both English and Spanish, through the world-wide syndicate of the National Catholic Welfare Conference. In order that the record, outlining the steps which led to the writing of the present book, may be complete, I am quoting from this Christmas card and this article:

"The telling and retelling of the Christmas Story and the various interpretations of its message and its meaning are sources of perennial joy, from one generation to another. At least, I have found them so and I believe that my experience is by no means unusual. Indeed, while discussing the subject with an old friend, not long ago, she told me about an incident which seemed to me both touching and provocative.

" 'I was trying to tell my little granddaughter the story of the Nativity,' this lady informed me. 'And the child kept saying, "But I don't understand why Mary and Joseph had to go to a stable.". . . 'Don't you see,' I repeated, 'there was no room for them at the inn. I said that before, darling. And they needed shelter. That's why they went to the stable.

" 'The child looked more and more bewildered and she began to look troubled, too. "I still don't understand," she said again, and this time her voice trembled a little, "Why didn't they go to Grandma's?" ' "

"I have recalled this story many times since then and each time it evokes several different thoughts. Of course I know that Joseph left Nazareth, where he plied his trade as a carpenter, and went to Bethlehem, the City of David, because 'all went to be enrolled, every one into his own city' and Joseph was 'of the house and family of David.' It was probably requisite, and certainly natural, that 'Mary, his espoused wife' should go with him. But I do not know why St. Anne did not go, too.

"The Church teaches us that she and her husband, Joachim, like Joseph, belonged to the House of David and, in this case, Bethlehem was her 'own city' no less than his. But Scripture does not mention her, in this connection or any other; so perhaps it is not strange that I know very little about St. Anne, even though her cult is an old one. I realize that she was supremely favored because she was the mother of Mary and that she must have been worthy of this favor in the sight of God. I have been to the house in Nazareth which was hers and where the Annunciation took place—at least, according to tradition; I have also been to the shrine in Canada which is the scene of many miracles attributed to her, the authenticity of which I do not doubt. I have read that she is the Patroness of Brittany, whose most illustrious queen was her namesake, and that she is often 'invoked by women in childbirth.' And I have seen countless modern and rather mediocre statues representing her with her daughter, whom she is teaching to read. These statues, far from inspiring me, have always caused me to wonder why the figure of St. Anne is so very tall in comparison to the Virgin Mary's—a child old enough to read is not so short that it does not reach its mother's waist. To be sure, I have also seen a few wonderful paintings of St. Anne by glorious old masters which show her with the Virgin and Child, these have done a great deal to offset the effect of the statues, both because they are so beautiful in themselves and because they give the impression of a happy and united family life, unshadowed by future sorrows—though apparently she was already a widow, since St. Joachim never appears in them. But it was not until I heard the puzzled child's query that I began to visualize St. Anne primarily in her capacity of a grandmother and to think of her with questioning sympathy.

"If she stayed at home in Nazareth when Mary, who was 'with child,' went to Bethlehem, wasn't she very anxious about her daughter and very eager to learn about the new baby? Did she hear the 'good tidings of great joy,' if not directly from the angels, then from some kindly neighbor who came back to Nazareth before Mary and Joseph? Did the Star in the East shed its light far enough for her to see? Did her first anxiety mount to anguish when she learned about the Slaughter of the Innocents? Was she very lonely while her daughter was in Egypt? Did Jesus spend much time with her in the little house where the angel had announced His coming? Did she invite John to stay there, too, so that the small cousins would be company for each other? Was it she who taught Jesus to read? Did she live long enough to see Him 'advanced in wisdom and age and grace with God and men.'

"These are some of the questions which I ask myself about St. Anne, as I make my Christmas preparations. For I do so nowadays largely in my own capacity as a grandmother; and I believe that no one—not even the little child to whom the Christmas celebration is still his most thrilling experience—has greater cause for rejoicing on this day of days than the mature woman to whom the revelation of the Nativity seems more wonderful every year. I say this with the blessed knowledge that

the most seemingly solitary Christmas need never be lonely for me—
or for any other human being—to whom the Child of Bethlehem has
become 'a living bright reality.'

"He must have been very real to St. Anne, even if she was alone in
Nazareth when He was born in Bethlehem. I do not doubt that she
can make Him very real to all of us, on His birthday, if we ask for this
grace with trustful and humble hearts."

The response to the article was even more overwhelming than the
response to the card and, this time, I was not only astonished; I was
appalled as well. I had started out merely to share a touching little
story, told me by one of my friends, with other friends, and this had
led to the writing of an article which had appeared in several languages
—for it found its way into French, too—in many parts of the world.
Now this in turn had led to a demand for a book; and what I had said,
both on my Christmas card and in my article, was all too true: I knew
very little about St. Anne. To be sure, I had great veneration for her,
but this was based on an illuminating personal experience at the Shrine
of Ste. Anne de Beaupré,[2] near Quebec, and I had never thought to
enlarge on it or investigate other reasons for such veneration; it had
always seemed to me perfect and complete just as it was. Now, though
it still seemed perfect as far as it went, it ceased to seem complete. I
realized that the demand for the book on St. Anne would mean extra
research, study, travelling and writing, when my working schedule
was already far too crowded for comfort; but I also realized it was one
with which I could not conscientiously decline to comply. The work of
a Catholic author is, or should be, an essential part of his Catholic
Action. It is an obligation he cannot escape.

So I have undertaken the extra research and study, the extra travelling and writing. And I have had my reward. Books about St. Anne are
hard to come by; but they exist and they form a treasure trove. Among
them are *The Lost Gospels*, which have much of the same dignity and
simple beauty as the canonical books; *The Golden Legend* of Jacques de
Voragines; *L'Aïeule du Christ: Sainte Anne de Jérusalem*; and *Les
Trois Légendes de Madame Saincte Anne*—all of them works calculated
to enrich immeasurably the minds of their readers, through the enlarge-
ment of their literary knowledge, besides uplifting their hearts. And

there is no lack of paintings and statues with which to clarify these writings; on the contrary, they abound in every part of the world which I have visited and many I have not. In the United States alone, there are nearly 400 Catholic churches dedicated to St. Anne and many Episcopal churches; in addition, both here and abroad, there are countless shrines and altars dedicated to her which interpret her cult and authenticate the reasons for it; and this veneration extends to the Greek Orthodox Church and the Church of England. She is the patron saint of both the Province of Quebec and the Province of Brittany and their shrines are perhaps the most famous and numerous;[3] and I was interested to discover that, whereas in Canada she is nearly always called La Bonne Sainte Anne, the Bretons hail her primarily as "Our Lord's Grandmother."[4] Other Christian localities and countries where she is especially honored are Apt in Provence—traditionally the site of her tomb—Annaberg and Rosenberg in Silesia, Bottelaere in Flanders, Düren and Aix-la-Chapelle in the Rhineland, and throughout Spain, where the family unit still remains supreme, and where St. Anne is logically considered the matriarch of the one we regard as Holy. The Spaniards have an old saying to the effect that if there is one person among them who has more power than a mother it is a grandmother; and I cannot recall a single city in their wonderful country where I have not found St. Anne represented as such. Perhaps my favorite image of her, however, is the primitive "miraculous statue," which has been enshrined in the Convent of Santa Aña at Avila ever since 1555. (The same con-

Miraculous statue of St. Anne, Convent of Santa Ana, Avila.

The Holy Family. Artist unknown. Dominican Convent, Madrigal.

vent, incidentally, where Isabella the Catholic sought and found sanctuary from her wicked brother, Henry, and where the Crown of Castile was offered to her.) But there are many other representations of which I am very fond: for instance, the painting of the entire Holy Family in the Dominican Convent at Madrigal, which was Isabella's birthplace; the statue which forms part of the reredos in the cathedral at Malaga, where St. Anne holds the Virgin and the Virgin the Christ Child—a treatment prevalent throughout Spain, though this was the first I happened to see; and the altarpiece in the Church of St. Anne at Granada where she and St. Joachim are shown in adoration on either side of the Virgin of the Immaculate Conception.

Nor are the places where St. Anne is singled out for homage limited to Christian countries. There is a church bearing her name on the site of her home, in what is now the Arab Section of Jerusalem, which, for years, has been directed by the French White Fathers to whom the property has been formally ceded; there are missions bearing her name at Fujieda in Japan and at Basutoland in South Africa; and there are shrines of St. Anne at Istanbul and Trebizond in Turkey and at Talavila in Ceylon. Indeed, I could go on and on, giving countless examples of the world wide veneration in which she is held.

And these examples would not all be of world famous shrines or statues or paintings, or missions that have found a foothold in places otherwise unillumined by the Light of the World. I have met many individuals whose devotion to St. Anne, though wholly unpublicized, has taken touching and lovely forms. Among these, I may mention Mary Stewart French of the State Department in Washington who, wandering one day in the Flea Market of Mexico City, came upon an isolated figurine which she divined, rather than knew, was meant to represent St. Anne. Yes, she was right, the vendor whom she questioned told her in reply; the figurine had been one of many included in a *nacimiento;* but the purchaser of the others had not cared for this one. (Who knows? Perhaps he did not feel it belonged in the Nativity scene along with the Mother and Child, the foster father, the shepherds, the wise men, the humble sheep and donkeys and oxen, the arrogant camels in their splendid trappings. After all, as I have said

Polychromed wooden figure of St. Anne.

before, there is no record of a grandmother's presence there!) The vendor had consented, after some pretty shrewd bargaining, to having all the others taken away and this one item left behind. There was something almost grotesque, as well as wholly pathetic, about the little figure; obviously, it must once have been provided with some sort of a seat, for it was carved in a sitting position. Miss French could not bear to leave it there, alone and unequipped. She bought it for the proverbial song—after all, the vendor was glad to be rid of it, for to him it had lost all meaning—and tenderly took it away. Once she had it safe in her home, she set about finding a bench for it; and, still not satisfied, she made, with her own hands, a small brocaded cushion to fit the bench. On this, St. Anne, now seated as befits her station and sanctity, occupies a place of honor among Mary French's numerous treasure!

I am glad that my research has unearthed such stories as these; and I am glad that my travelling has taken me back to Ste. Anne de Beaupré and given me the answers to the questions I should have asked long ago; that it has taken me to the Shrine of St. Anne on Ile La Motte, in Lake Champlain, where I had never been before, though I have lived in Vermont so much of my life. (And though I pride myself on being something of a student of history, I never knew before that this marked not only the site of the first Mass said in New England, but of the first settlement—1666—in what is now Vermont.) I am glad that it has taken me to the little village of Milford, not far, on the mainland, from Isle La Motte—a village in a region regarded as a stronghold of Protestantism where one of those many churches dedicated to St. Anne on

Marker at St. Anne's Shrine. Isle La Motte. Vermont.

Shrine of St. Anne, Milford, Vermont.

American soil is located; a church moreover which is the proud pos-
sessor of two authentic relics and the scene of undisputed miracles of
healing, as the crutches and canes beside the altar testify. I am glad
that it has taken me to the Shrine of St. Ann in New Orleans, where
there is an Archconfraternity bearing her name. I am glad that it has
taken me to the austerely beautiful church of St. Anne and its walled
inclosure, in Jerusalem, on the site of the traditional home of Anne and
her husband, Joachim: a lovely peaceful flowering place, untouched
by the turmoil which, in recent years, alas! has raged around it. I am
glad that it has taken me to Apt, the quiet cathedral town in Provence,
so strangely overlooked by visitors to nearby Arles and Avignon, where
the mortal remains of St. Anne were hidden away from the vandals,
and rediscovered, centuries later, by the Great Charlemagne himself,
to whom much of the subsequent cult of St. Anne was henceforth due.
I am glad that it has taken me to Ste. Anne d'Auray, on the greatest of
all Breton festivals, to have a small part in the pilgrimage on St. Anne's

St. Anne with the Virgin. Benzoni. St. Anne's Cathedral, Apt.

feast day. I am glad that in all these places, I have been privileged to talk with persons who have devoted their lives to a study of St. Anne and who were ready and willing to share their knowledge with me.

And the extra writing? That, I must confess, has been harder— much harder than the research and study, harder even than the travelling, though a good deal of that has been undertaken with various handicaps to pleasant and easy progress. As I have remarked before, Ernie Pyle was right when he said, "There is no easy way to do your work. However, it may seem to you, writing is an exhausting and tearing thing." It becomes doubly so when the labor of doing it is added to a heavy output, already promised for a definite time, and an inescapable sense of inadequacy in performing an important and significant task. But I have been supported by the firm belief that it was not thrust upon me accidentally or hastily, but as part of a pattern which, in turn, forms an essential part of my life. So, as I have said, I have already had my reward; and I shall have it in still greater measure if the result of my labors takes the form of more general consciousness that

Our Lord Had a Grandmother, Too.

PART I.

The Life of St. Anne

Tree of Jesse. Tapestry, Reims Cathedral.

I

"The Blessed and Ever Glorious Virgin Mary, sprung from the royal race and family of David, was born in the city of Nazareth, educated at Jerusalem, in the Temple of the Lord.

"Her father's name was Joachim and her mother's Anna. The family of her father was of Galilee and the city of Nazareth. The family of her mother was of Bethlehem.

"Their lives were plain and right in the sight of the Lord, pious and faultless before men."

These are the lines, beautiful in their simplicity and clarity, with which the Gospel of the Birth of Mary, one of the so-called "lost" books of the Bible, begins. These "lost" books, more than a score in number, and not infrequently approximating, in certain passages, the text of the Gospels, the Acts and the Epistles, were omitted from the various authorized translations of the New Testament; but though they are not canonical, they are, indubitably, of great antiquity. The Gospel of the Birth of Mary is attributed to St. Matthew, and it was certainly considered authentic by many of the early Christians. I do not know of any reason why we should hesitate to so consider it, too, in the main, even if we decide to accept the verdict of those chroniclers who maintain that Mary was born, as well as educated, in Jerusalem. But when we go further back into the story of St. Anne, we must admittedly depend on tradition and legend, folksong and vision.

As a matter of fact, I do not know why we should hesitate to do this, either. I shall never forget the good counsel once given me by a wise and understanding Mexican cleric. "We Catholics have two priceless treasures," he reminded me, "a treasure of gold and a treasure of silver. Our treasure of gold lies in the Scriptures and Divine Tradition, on which our Church is founded; these we are bound to believe. Our treasure of silver lies in the popular traditions, which we may accept or not, as we choose, but we are nearly always the happier for having done so." Granted that the stories describing the earlier part of St. Anne's life are sometimes confusing because they are slightly contradictory and that they seem to range in fields of fantasy, rather than to be set on the solid foundations of fact, they are believable as to background, charming as to setting and symbolic as to message; rightfully, they deserve an honored place in our silver treasure. I have pored over them reverently as well as studiously; and I feel that their conflicting elements are relatively unimportant, and that whether their fantastic elements should be explained, at least they can and should be interpreted. So here are the results of my prayerful effort to do so:

Early in the century before the Christian Era, a patriarchal family belonging to the tribe of Levi took refuge on the barren plateaus at the north of Galilee. The little group had not voluntarily left the pasture lands of their natural habitation; they were refugees from the conquering hordes of Romans which had swept over Palestine and brought it under the rigid rule of Caesar. They eked out a bare existence in the desert; but the wild grapes and figs on which they tried to subsist, and the rude huts and caves which formed their shelters were little to their liking. They missed their flocks and their fields and their well-ordered homes in the villages that adjoined their pastures so much that, as soon as they dared, they went cautiously back to the towns surrounded by fertile meadows from which they had come. By tradition, their way of life was nomadic as well as pastoral, however. So the necessity of continued movement, imposed by continued wars and rumors of wars, was not a great hardship and they did not always remain in or near the same village. It is not clear just when they went from one to another, but among those where their chief[5] and his wife made their home were Sephoris, Bethlehem and Hebron.

The elder daughter of this couple, Hismarian, was apparently born in Sephoris; but when she was eight years old, and her little sister, Anne, was born, they may have already gone on to Bethlehem. It does not greatly matter. Both were lovely little villages, set in a green countryside and surrounded by mountains; in both, the flat roof of the better houses served, to a large degree, as it still does, for the family living room, except during the heat of midday in summer and the cool of the evening in winter. The furnishings of these houses were simple, almost sparse according to our modern standards; and very often the rocky surface of the mountainside formed their rear walls, at least in part, giving them a certain cave-like quality, such as may still be seen in many houses, not only of that region, but also in Spain, France and doubtless elsewhere in regions with which I am unfamiliar. But there was a tranquility and a graciousness in the way of life among those who inhabited them. They were not needy people and, for the most part, they were not ignorant people, partly because their needs were few, and partly because they were frugal, provident and studious. But they made a virtue of hospitality, and their family life was harmonious; children were brought up to honor their father and their mother, and not only to learn, but to keep, all the Commandments. Their general education included the Law and the Prophets.

This is the sort of atmosphere in which Anne's mother grew up. Like every normal Jewish girl of her time, she looked forward to early marriage and abundant maternity; and like every Jewish girl nurtured in the fear and admonition of the Lord, she was watchfully waiting for the coming of the Messiah, whose birth had been foretold by the Prophets, and had cherished the hope that she might be His mother. Before her marriage, she had visited a hermit, highly reputed for holiness, who had told her that, though she would not have a son, she would have a daughter, who in turn would give birth to a "most holy virgin, even the future mother of God." It was natural that, after this, she should wait for some experience of her own that would seem to confirm the prophecy, and watch for special signs of favor from heaven in her first born, a girl named Hismarian. But up to the time this elder daughter was married to Eliud, a young neighbor, no such signs had appeared; nor did they do so when Hismarian, the year after her early marriage, gave birth to a daughter whom they called Elizabeth.

With Anne, it was different. Her mother had almost given up hope of having a second child when one evening, as she was kneeling in prayer on her housetop, she thought she saw a strange light. Soon this light seemed to encircle her like fire and out of the air came a "clamorous sound" which gradually took the form of words, repeating the hermit's promise. At almost the same hour, her husband, who was still in the fields with his flock, beheld a fiery cloud; and from it came a mighty voice telling him that, on his return to his home, he would find written upon his couch four letters which had not been placed there by the hand of man, and that these letters would form the name of the child which should be born to his wife through the will of God.

The vision faded, leaving the quietude of twilight over the peaceful meadow. The shepherd hurried home and entered his bedchamber. His wife was there before him, kneeling in wonderment beside the couch on which A-N-N-A was written in letters of gold.

The meaning of the word, in Hebrew, is grace. Neither husband nor wife doubted that their joint vision had a celestial origin or that their next child would be the mother of a "holy virgin" and the grandmother of the Messiah.

II

The miraculous manifestations continued, and everything about the birth of their baby seemed propitious and significant to her happy parents.

The golden letters, spelling the name Anna, appeared in various other parts of the room besides their couch and were imprinted on their little daughter's breast. They kept this partially uncovered, so that the crowds that came to see her might share their wonder and their hope. Among the throng were hermits from Carmel, shepherds from the fields, neighbors from the village; and there was one stranger from Nazareth, a man of wealth and distinction named Seral, who could not see the golden letters, for he had been blind from birth. But he came with faith and, entering the room where the child lay at her mother's side, asked that the baby's tiny hands might be placed in his. When this had been done, he moved them gently, so that they would cover his eyes, and said with confident earnestness, "Daughter of God, open my eyes, that I may behold the wonders wrought by you in heaven.". . . "And immediately he saw and praised God for his wonders."[6]

So, even in her infancy, Anne's work of healing, which has gone on through the centuries since her life and death, had already begun. But there is nothing to indicate that the excitement which surrounded her birth continued indefinitely. On the contrary, though authorities disagree as to where she spent her childhood and her youth, they seem agreed that it was peaceful as well as pleasant.

According to some of these stories, her parents moved to Nazareth while she was still very young, but parted from Anne and placed her in the temple at Jerusalem for her upbringing and education. According to others—and these are the same that give Bethlehem and Hebron as temporary abiding places of the family—the household moved to Jerusalem when Anne was nine years old—that is, shortly after her elder sister's marriage—and went to live near the temple where her father had been summoned to take a permanent position, in recognition of the sacerdotal services performed by his ancestors as well as of his own worth. Profiting by his connection there, he entrusted the education of his daughter to the scribes who were among his friends and later, to certain doctors of the Law. But his duties did not interfere with the periods that he still spent among his flocks. Like other Levites, he had the inherent right to a tract of land a thousand paces wide outside the city and, little by little, he acquired additional plots; and when he went into the country to oversee his pasture land, he took his little daughter with him.

This is the version of the story that I like best and that seems to me most plausible. Hismarian, the elder daughter of the devout couple, was undoubtedly married when Anne was still a little girl; it would have been natural for them to keep the younger one at home, especially as, by so doing, she could have all the privileges of an urban dwelling and a good education at the temple, because of her father's connection with it, but without going to live there; she could also have had the advantage of country life which he was able to give her.[7]

From the terrace of her home, she could look out on the shrines at the south and, above the fortifications at the east, she could gaze on a horizon which offered a series of wonders. First, gazing downward, she would see the Valley of Cedron, so called because of the cedars which bordered the stream which flowed through it; then, glancing upward, the Mount of Olives; farther off, on a vast expanse, the tableland and mountain ranges that rose before the Dead Sea; still more distant, envisioned rather than beheld, the Mountain of Moab from which Moses, before he drew his last breath, had been allowed his one fleeting, rewarding glimpse of the Promised Land.

Such were the sights that met the eyes and warmed the heart of Anne as a child. Also, since she went often with her father to see his cherished flocks, she came to know the green pastures, freshened by many still, small pools and by the gushing spring of Silöe. All around her, the fields of wheat, of barley, of lentils; then verdant oaks and sycamores, groves of pines, orchards of olive trees; everywhere, at intervals, fig trees clustering closely around nearby rocks. In the midst of this pleasant landscape, giving it life and meaning, were straggling cattle, small flocks of sheep with a few goats scattered among them and, climbing the steep paths of the thyme-scented hills, countless sure-footed donkeys. Last, but not least, from time to time, a caravan of camels wound its way majestically across the bright plains.

But this animated beauty of the fields absorbed only part of Anne's attention. She learned the history and geography of Israel, mathematics, natural sciences in as far as they were then recognized and studied— in short, the practical and familiar arts, all leading, as they should, to the greater glory of God. She learned how the universe came into being, or rather, the world in its relation to the universe. This mystery was represented, at that era, in the form of seven tableaux, representing seven days—the origin of the week's division. She learned of God's plans for His people—her people—and the fulfillment of these plans from the time of the creation; the calling of Abraham; the foundation of the twelve tribes of Israel; the reign of David, that great king destined to be the forefather of the Messiah. She learned astronomy and, through her study of the sky, the division of the year into months: Schedat, Adar, Nisan, Iyar, Sivan, Tamonz, Ab, Elloul, Tishri, Hesvan, Kisler and Tebeth. Above all, she learned to remember the Sabbath Day and keep it holy.

But none of this advanced education interfered with practical household duties. These were so well organized, however, that they were never an interference or a burden. The day began, as it ended, with prayer. Then Anne helped her mother prepare the simple dishes that made up their daily fare and learned to draw wine, with the aid of a small vessel, from the great jars placed where they would become cool. She went to fetch water from the well, with her young companions, just as her noble ancestress, Rebecca, had done. And when the last duty was performed and the last prayer said, she extinguished the flame of her tiny oil lamp and lay down to sleep on her narrow bed.

She was lovely, she was learned, she was discreet and reverent. No wonder that among a people where these qualities were held in high esteem she was early sought in marriage.

St. Anne. Anonymous.

III

She had the natural inclination for it and the careful preparation for it characteristic of her time and race. It had never occurred to her that in due course she would not marry, and that her marriage would not be a lasting and happy one, based on mutual affection and respect. To be sure, there were certain laws among the Jews, theoretically strict, which forbade marriage outside their own tribes, except under very special conditions; but young people of both sexes met frequently and pleasantly, under proper supervision; and Anne apparently had little or no difficulty in making a choice as satisfactory to herself as it was both to her parents and to those of the young man who had found favor in her sight.

He was generally called Joachim, and that is the name by which he has become known to posterity; but he was also called Heliakim, frequently shortened to Heli.[8] Like his wife's, his name seems peculiarly significant, for it means Preparation for the Saviour. He had a younger brother, Jacob, and they were the sons of a certain Mathas, who lived in Nazareth, and who was an old friend of Anne's parents. After the latter moved to Jerusalem, Mathas continued to visit them and to bring his children with him. Evidently both fathers had long considered a union between their respective families a desirable objective; for though they were not of the same tribe, the special conditions which permitted a departure from established custom were not lacking. Although Joachim, as the eldest son of Mathas, who belonged to the tribe of Judah, had the rights of primogeniture, it was presumable that his younger brother, Jacob, could fulfill the tribal law designed partly to safeguard inheritance and partly to insure perpetuity.[9] Anne's family belonged to the tribe of Levi, and her elder sister, Hismarian, had married into that tribe, so the requirements of the same law had already been fulfilled; and since, according to the Prophets, it was from the tribe of Judah that the promised Messiah was to come, Anne's parents who, like all other devout Jews of the period, hoped that a daughter of theirs might be the chosen mother of Emmanuel, were overjoyed to see in their younger child a possible channel for the fulfillment of the prophecy.

It is safe to assume that the marriage of Joachim and Anne, who were then both probably about twenty years old—Joachim a little older, Anne a little younger—followed established custom, as their betrothal had done. Mathas would have come down from Nazareth, accompanied by all the members of his family; Anne's sister, Hismarian, would have come from Hebron, with her husband and their daughter, Elizabeth— quite a big girl by now; other relatives, near and far, both as to distance and kinship, would have foregathered; and all day long there would have been singing and general merry-making in the bride's house. But she would have taken no part in this. Instead, she would have remained secluded in her room until it was time for her to leave her home and go to the temple where the marriage ceremony was to take place. Early in the morning she had bathed in fresh water and been annointed with fragrant oils before she was dressed in her wedding garments: a long violet colored robe, embroidered in flowers, with sandals embroidered to match. But it was not until evening that her two maids of honor covered her beautifully dressed hair with the long violet colored veil which floated out behind her like a mantle and placed the nuptial crown above it. When she had thus been prepared to greet her bride-groom, he arrived to claim her, accompanied by ten chosen companions, who announced his approach by the music they made on their fifes and tambours. Anne's bridesmaids had also assembled—ten young girls, each carrying a lighted lamp in one hand and a sprig of myrtle in the other. Preceded by their double cortege, the bride and groom went hand in hand to the temple and took their places on the dais that had been prepared for them.

The ceremony began with the reading, by a scribe, of the marriage contract, complete in every detail. This was done under the supervision of a priest, attired in gorgeous vestments. After the reading of the con-tract came the bestowal of the wedding ring. Next Anne was handed a cup, full to the brim, which she passed to Joachim; after drinking from it, he gave it back to her and she drank in her turn. Then she threw it to the ground, where it broke into glittering fragments. This was the symbol of conjugal unity, shared misfortunes as well as shared joys, which brought the formal religious ceremony to an end.

Night had now come on, and the young men of Joachim's cortege carried torches to light the way through the dark streets from the temple to the flower decked room where the wedding supper was set forth. The occasion was still one of great solemnity. Not until seven nuptial benedictions had been pronounced, could the guests relax on the divans surrounding the table; and after each course, ritual ablutions took place. In between, there was laughing and drinking and jesting, along with the feasting. But the supper ended with still another benediction; and when this had been pronounced, the guests began to disperse. The light from the torches was fainter now; it no longer flared into flame, but flickered as it sank into the sockets. The music from the fifes and tambours sounded more and more softly and died away in the distance. All had gone their separate ways, quietly, into the night.

All except Joachim and Anne, who remained behind, together.

Royal Museum of Fine Arts, Brussels Copyright, A. C. L. Bruxelles.

Parents of St. Anne. C. von Coninxloo.

IV

It had been agreed between Joachim's father and Anne's that the young couple should remain in Jerusalem. As has already been said, Joachim, an eldest son, had the rights of primogeniture, but his younger brother, Jacob, was entirely capable of giving Mathas all the help required in looking after his property in Nazareth, whereas Anne's father had no son to share the responsibility of caring for his ever increasing flocks, while he himself was more and more occupied with his duties at the temple. His other son-in-law, Hismarian's husband, was too far away—for Hebron then seemed a distant place. It was natural that Joachim should fit easily into the patriarchal picture.

The arrangement, from the first, was both profitable and harmonious. The flocks continued to increase; more pasture land was added to the fertile fields which had already assured the family of abundance; and Joachim and Anne were established in a pleasant house set down in a flowering garden, close to the city walls and to a pool known as Bethesda, which the populace believed had healing powers and which, indubitably, was a source of refreshment and a place of repose.

The years flowed on, peacefully and, for the most part, uneventfully, except for the faithful observance of all traditional feasts and fasts, which differed in its details, but not in its essentials from the observance of these same feasts and fasts kept by Orthodox Jews in our own day. Every week, the Sabbath was strictly set aside as a day of rest. In the month of Adar (February) came the Feast of Purim, commemorating the deliverance of the Jews from the massacre planned by Haman[10]; and, at this time, the population of Jerusalem was in holiday mood, and Joachim and Anne joined in the general evidences of lighthearted rejoicing. In the month of Nisan (March) came the Passover, with the temporary cessation of all work, the sacrifice of the Paschal Lamb, and other solemn ceremonials which had remained unchanged since the

Children of Israel had escaped from Egypt; this was a feast of especial significance to Anne, since it was her ancestor, Aaron, the elder brother of Moses, who had been the spokesman for the Jews at the court of the hard-hearted Pharaoh. Following Yom Kippur—the day of expiation— and falling in the same month of Tishri (September) came the Feast of the Tabernacle, lasting eight days. During this festival, tents were erected everywhere—in the fields, on the terraces, even in the public squares of the city—to recall the long period of probation passed by the Jews in the desert, and the intervention of God in their behalf. Meanwhile, every morning, a priest went to the fountain of Silöe, to draw from it water in a golden vessel and, returning to the temple, to pour this over the sacrifice on the altar, symbolizing the "living waters" of promise.

All these festivals were beautiful in themselves and beautiful in their symbolism; they served as landmarks in the passage of the quiet years, uneventful, as we have said, for the most part. Joachim and Anne were fond of both books and music; in the evenings, they read together, or Anne sang while her husband accompanied her on the harp. Their tastes were so congenial, their lives so harmonious, that they had little need for many outside diversions; and besides, when night came, they were ready for rest. Joachim continued to give the ever increasing flocks his personal attention and supervision; this took him into the fields every day and kept him there until darkness fell. Anne continued to oversee the household, to work in her garden, to sew and spin. Flowers flourished under her care, and her garments, though simple in cut, were of many colored fabrics, skilfully draped and becomingly worn. At need, she went out into the city to do her marketing and other necessary errands, and she was faithful in her attendance at the temple and on the poor. She had a great gift of nursing the sick of both body and mind, and those in pain and distress frequently called on her for help and were never denied. She showed a special skill in her care for women, and more than once helped a midwife at the time of a difficult birth or officiated in place of one who failed to arrive.

All this she did not only as part of her duty, but gladly, welcoming it as a way in which she could serve her fellow creatures and, through them, her God. No one ever felt that her help was given grudgingly. But it was in her own home that she was happiest. The streets were full of Roman soldiers, arrogant and overbearing; she shrank, instinctively, from these cruel alien rulers of her beloved country. Hoards of wretched beggars clustered in the public places where they were segregated, calling aloud on the pity of the passer-by. Anne did what she could to relieve their misery, which haunted her otherwise happy life; but she was all too conscious of her own inadequacy. It would take one greater and stronger than she to deliver them from their wretchedness.

In the early years of her marriage, the patriarchal group to which Anne and Joachim belonged was a large one, congenial and mutually helpful. Its members gathered together frequently, for both business and pleasure. Then the elder members of both families died, one by one, and their loss brought sorrow to the younger ones who had loved them; but it was a sorrow softened by the memory of their parents' long, full, useful lives and the knowledge that the years of all men's lives are numbered. But there was another sorrow which could not be assuaged; this was their own childlessness.

We have said before, and it cannot be too strongly stressed, that the heart's desire of every normal young Jew was for an early, suitable, happy and lasting marriage; and coupled with this desire was another, equally strong: that the marriage should be fruitful. The merits attributable to celibacy became evident only with the dawn of Christianity, when the early followers of Jesus discovered that in order to consecrate their lives entirely to His service, and to help others along the way of truth, there should be no earthly ties or distractions to hinder their greatest purposes. As for the theory that a childless marriage left a couple freer to pursue their own selfish ways, that was, happily, many centuries in the future.

> "Blessed art thou, and it shall be well with thee.
> Thy wife as a fruitful vine, on the sides of thy house.
> Thy children as olive plants, round about thy table.
> Behold, thus shall the man be blessed that feareth the Lord."

Such had been the pronouncements of Joachim's ancestor, the great King David, and their truth had never been questioned in all the centuries that had passed since the declaration had been made. The woman who had never conceived, the man who had never begotten, felt an inheritance to be incomplete, a blessing to be limited. More than this: they felt that their childlessness was a punishment for something they had done which they ought not to have done, or something they had left undone that they ought to have done. They dreaded the moment of public reproach and public humiliation so often meted out to the childless. Anne and Joachim were no exception to this universal rule.

But at the particular period of Jewish history which had now been reached, in the families belonging to the tribe of Judah, this sorrowful feeling of unfulfillment was greater than it had ever been before, and greater than it was among other families, even then. None doubted that Judah was the tribe to which would be granted the unique and supreme honor of giving the Messiah to the world; and every prophecy, every portent, pointed to the fact that the hour of His coming was not far distant.[11]

It is safe to say that in our own day and age there is hardly a mother, who has given thought to her children's future, who has not hoped that her sons and daughters would be pre-eminently successful, in whatever terms she interpreted success. The more thoughtful, the more conscientious, the more cultured, have allowed their hopes to soar even higher, and have striven and sacrificed, if necessary, to realize these. It should therefore be easy for nearly all mothers to understand how much higher still must have soared the hopes of those who believed themselves qualified by birth to provide a Deliverer for their people, and whose whole pattern of life was planned in such a way as to make them worthy of this privilege if it should come to them. When month after month and year after year went by without the prospect of a child, Anne must inevitably have had moments of feeling that her prayers had gone not only unanswered but unheard; she must have asked herself why she and her husband, who had so scrupulously followed the Law, should thus be punished; she must have dreaded increasingly the moment when their private grief would become a public disgrace.

I could, of course, attempt to tell you in my own way what finally happened. But it has been told with such infinite beauty in the Gospel of the Birth of Mary—one of the so-called "lost" books of the Bible— and in the Protevangelium of St. James the Less that I prefer to quote it, exactly as it was written centuries ago. No words that I could put on paper could possibly tell this part of the story as vividly, as poignantly, and as exquisitely.

"And it came to pass, that when the feast of the dedication drew near, Joachim, with some others of his tribe, went up to Jerusalem, and at that time, Issachar was high-priest;

"Who, when he saw Joachim along with the rest of his neighbours, bringing his offering, despised both him and his offerings, and asked him,

"Why he, who had no children, would presume to appear among those who had? Adding, that his offerings could never be acceptable to God, who was judged by him unworthy to have children; the Scripture having said, Cursed is every one who shall not beget a male in Israel.

"He further said, that he ought first to be free from that curse by begetting some issue, and then come with his offerings into the presence of God.

"But Joachim being much confounded with the shame of such reproach, retired to the shepherds, who were with the cattle in their pastures;

"For he was not inclined to return home, lest his neighbours, who were present and heard all this from the high-priest, should publicly reproach him in the same manner. . . . .

"But when he had been there for some time, on a certain day when he was alone, the angel of the Lord stood by him with a prodigious light.

"To whom, being troubled at the appearance, the angel who had appeared to him, endeavouring to compose him said:

"Be not afraid, Joachim, nor troubled at the sight of me, for I am an angel of the Lord sent by him to you, that I might inform you, that your prayers are heard, and your alms ascended in the sight of God.

"For he hath surely seen your shame, and heard you unjustly reproached for not having children: for God is the avenger of sin, and not of nature;

"And so when he shuts the womb of any person, he does it for this reason, that he may in a more wonderful manner again open it, and that which is born appear to be not the product of lust, but the gift of God.

"For the first mother of your nation, Sarah, was she not barren even till her eightieth year: and yet even in the end of her old age brought forth Isaac, in whom the promise was made a blessing to all nations.

"Rachel also, so much in favour with God, and beloved so much by holy Jacob, continued barren for a long time, yet afterwards was the mother of Joseph, who was not only governor of Egypt, but delivered many nations from perishing with hunger.

"Who among the judges was more valiant than Samson, or more holy than Samuel? And yet both their mothers were barren.

"But if reason will not convince you of the truth of my words, that there are frequent conceptions in advanced years, and that those who were barren have brought forth to their great surprise; therefore Anna your wife shall bring you a daughter, and you shall call her name Mary;

"She shall, according to your vow, be devoted to the Lord from her infancy, and be filled with the Holy Ghost from her mother's womb;

"She shall neither eat nor drink anything which is unclean, nor shall her conversation be without among the common people, but in the temple of the Lord; that so she may not fall under any slander or suspicion of what is bad.

"So in the process of her years, as she shall be in a miraculous manner born of one that was barren, so she shall, while yet a virgin, in a way unparalleled, bring forth the Son of the most High God, who shall be called Jesus, and, according to the signification of his name, be the Saviour of all nations.

Story of St. Joachim and St. Anne. Gaudenzio Ferrari.

"And this shall be a sign to you of the things which I declare, namely, when you come to the golden gate of Jerusalem, you shall there meet your wife Anna, who being very much troubled that you returned no sooner, shall then rejoice to see you.

"When the angel had said this he departed from him. . . . .

"Afterwards the angel appeared to Anna his wife saying: Fear not, neither think that which you see is a spirit.

"For I am that angel who hath offered up your prayers and alms before God, and am now sent to you, that I may inform you, that a daughter will be born unto you, who shall be called Mary, and shall be blessed above all women.

"She shall be, immediately upon her birth, full of the grace of the Lord, and shall continue during the three years of her weaning in her father's house, and afterwards, being devoted to the service of the Lord, shall not depart from the temple, till she arrives to years of discretion.

"In a word, she shall there serve the Lord night and day in fasting and prayer, shall abstain from every unclean thing, and never know any man;

"But being an unparalleled instance without any pollutions or defilement, and a virgin not knowing any man, shall bring forth a son, and a maid shall bring forth the Lord, who both by his grace and name and works, shall be the Saviour of the world.

"Arise therefore, and go up to Jerusalem, and when you shall come to that which is called the golden gate (because it is gilt with gold), as a sign of what I have told you, you shall meet your husband, for whose safety you have been so very much concerned.

"When therefore you find these things thus accomplished, believe that all the rest which I have told you, shall also undoubtedly be accomplished.

"According therefore to the command of the angel, both of them left the places where they were, and when they came to the place specified in the angel's prediction, they met each other.

"Then, rejoicing at each other's vision, and being fully satisfied in

The Meeting of St. Anne and St. Joachim at the Golden Gate.
Master of Moulins.

the promise of a child, they gave due thanks to the Lord, who exalts the humble.

"After having praised the Lord, they returned home, and lived in a cheerful and assured expectation of the promise of God.

"So Anna conceived, and brought forth a daughter, and, according to the angel's command, the parents did call her the name Mary."

This is the story of the Virgin's conception and birth as it appears in the Gospel of the Birth of Mary; now for the story as it appears in the Protevangelium:

"In the history of the twelve tribes of Israel we read there was a certain person called Joachim, who being very rich, made double offerings to the Lord God, having made this resolution: my substance shall be for the benefit of the whole people, and that I may find mercy from the Lord God for the forgiveness of my sins.

"But at a certain great feast of the Lord, when the children of Israel offered their gifts, and Joachim also offered his, Reuben the high-priest opposed him, it is not lawful for thee to offer thy gifts, seeing thou hast not begot any issue in Israel.

"At this Joachim being concerned very much, went away to consult the registries of the twelve tribes, to see whether he was the only person who had begot no issue.

"But upon inquiry he found that all righteous had raised up seed in Israel:

"Then he called to mind the patriarch Abraham, How that God in the end of his life had given him his son Isaac; upon which he was exceedingly distressed, and would not be seen by his wife:

"But retired into the wilderness, and fixed his tent there, and fasted forty days and forty nights, saying to himself,

"I will not go down either to eat or drink, till the Lord my God shall look down upon me, but prayer shall be my meat and drink. . . . .

"In the meantime his wife Anna was distressed and perplexed on a double account, and said I will mourn both for my widowhood and my barrenness.

"Then drew near a great feast of the Lord, and Judith her maid said, How long will you thus afflict your soul? The feast of the Lord is now come, when it is unlawful for any one to mourn.

"Take therefore this hood which was given by one who makes such things, for it is not fit that I, who am a servant, should wear it, but it well suits a person of your great character.

"But Anna replied, Depart from me, I am not used to such things; besides, the Lord hath greatly humbled me.

"I feel some ill-designing person hath given thee this, and thou art come to pollute me with my sin.

"Then Judith her maid answered, What evil shall I wish you when you will not hearken to me?

"I cannot wish you a greater curse than you are under, in that God hath shut up your womb, that you should not be a mother in Israel.

"At this Anna was exceedingly troubled, and having on her wedding garment, went about three o'clock in the afternoon to walk in her garden.

"And she saw a laurel-tree, and sat under it, and prayed unto the Lord, saying,

"O God of my fathers, bless me and regard my prayer as thou didst bless the womb of Sarah, and gave her a son Isaac. . . . .

"And as she was looking towards heaven she perceived a sparrow's nest in the laurel.

"And mourning within herself, she said, Wo is me, who begat me? And what womb did bear me, that I should be thus accursed before the children of Israel, and that they should reproach and deride me in the temple of my God: Wo is me, to what can I be compared?

"I am not comparable to the very beasts of the earth, for even the beasts of the earth are fruitful before thee, O Lord! Wo is me, to what can I be compared?

"I am not comparable to the brute animals, for even the brute animals are fruitful before thee O Lord! Wo is me, to what am I comparable?

"I cannot be compared to these waters, for even the waters are fruitful before thee, O Lord! Wo is me, to what can I be compared?

"I am not comparable to the waves of the sea; for these, whether they are calm, or in motion, with the fishes which are in them, praise thee, O Lord! Wo is me, to what can I be compared?

"I am not comparable to the very earth, for the earth produces its fruits, and praises thee, O Lord! . . . .

"Then an angel of the Lord stood by her and said, Anna, the Lord hath heard thy prayer; thou shalt conceive and bring forth, and thy progeny shall be spoken of in all the world.

"And Anna answered, As the Lord my God liveth, whatever I bring forth, whether it be male or female, I will devote it to the Lord my God, and it shall minister to him in holy things, during its whole life.

"And behold there appeared two angels, saying unto her, Behold Joachim thy husband is coming with his shepherds.

"For an angel of the Lord hath also come down to him, and said, The Lord God hath heard thy prayer, make haste and go hence, for behold Anna thy wife shall conceive.

"And Joachim went down and called his shepherds, saying Bring me hither ten she-lambs without spot or blemish, and the twelve calves shall be for the priests and the elders.

"Bring me also a hundred goats, and the hundred goats shall be for the whole people.

"And Joachim went down with the shepherds, and Anna stood by the gate and saw Joachim coming with the shepherds.

"And she ran, and hanging about his neck, said, Now I know that the Lord hath greatly blessed me:

"For behold, I who was a widow am no longer a widow, and I who was barren shall conceive. . . . .

"And Joachim abode the first day in his house, but on the morrow he brought his offerings and said,

"If the Lord be propitious to me let the plate which is on the priest's forehead make it manifest.

"And he consulted the plate which the priest wore, and saw it, and behold sin was not found in him.

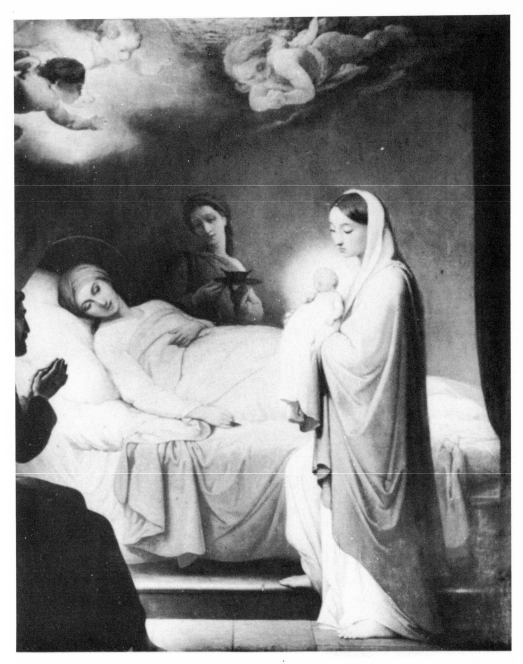

Nativity of Mary. Church of St. Séverin, Paris.

"And Joachim said, Now I know that the Lord is propitious to me, and hath taken away all my sins.

"And he went down from the temple of the Lord justified, and he went to his own house.

"And when nine months were fulfilled to Anna she brought forth, and said to the midwife, What have I brought forth?

"And she told her, a girl.

"Then Anna said, the Lord hath this day magnified my soul; and she laid her in bed.

"And when the days of her purification were accomplished, she gave suck to the child, and called her name Mary."

I am sure every reader of these beautiful passages will agree that it is in the words of the Gospel of the Birth of Mary and of the Prote-vangelium, so fortunately still available to us, that this part of St. Anne's story should be told, and that comment on it or expansion of it by any modern writer of limited ability would be not only presumptuous, but completely futile.

Nativity of the Virgin. After Murillo.

The Birth of the Virgin. Anonymous, 16th Century.

V

Neither the so-called Gospel of Pseudo-Matthew nor the Protevangelium of St. James the Less mentions the birthplace of the Virgin. But, as we have seen, the Gospel of the Birth of Mary, also attributed to St. Matthew, refers to this as Nazareth. The author gives no grounds for doing so, nor is there any reason why he should have—he was not trying to settle an argument, but to tell a simple and beautiful story, factual in as far as he knew the facts; and many reliable authorities not only accept his statement, but hotly defend it, giving all sorts of reasons, both convincing and unconvincing for doing so. On the other hand, countless equally reliable authorities contest the validity of the statement with even more fervor and bring forward their own claims to prove that the Virgin Mary was born in Jerusalem. The importance given to this debatable point, by almost every thoughtful chronicler of St. Anne's life, makes me feel that it must be discussed before continuing her story, loath as I am to interrupt a normal flow of narrative which treats of events in their natural order without confusing interruption. For this is not a case of presenting one item of the silver treasure, which we are free to accept or reject as we please; it is a case of presenting two items which seem to be contradictory, and asking the reader to take his choice between them—or, if he chooses, reject them both.

The claim in favor of Nazareth has been made by many writers, both ancient and modern, and has been supported by at least four Popes; it has been widely accepted throughout the Occident, though much less widely in the Orient. All this certainly entitles it to serious consideration, if not actually to the "pious belief" which at one time was encouraged, while not commanded, by Papal decree. But when it is analyzed, the claim is found to rest very largely on legend and sentiment. Of course there is the lovely story of the *Casa Santa*, borne by angels from Nazareth to Loretto, and still visited annually by thousands of devout pilgrims, whose belief that it is the house in which the Virgin was born always has remained and always will remain unshaken; and this belief is based on the affirmation contained in a Brief issued by Julian II. Many other lovely stories have been told by modern writers. One of these—Pincinelli—recalls that the name Nazareth means "City of Flowers" and concludes that since Mary has often been called the "Flower of Galilee," it follows that the Virgin came from Nazareth just as a lily comes from a flowering garden! Still another writer—Faber—embroiders his opinion in such poetical language that the reason for it is almost lost, and describes the Virgin's childhood home in this way:

"She was born, *according to the will of God,* amidst the holy hills of Palestine, at a time when this was still a land of milk and honey. Among all its provinces, Galilee is the most pleasant; and among the villages of Galilee, Nazareth blooms like a rose. There, at the foot of a great rock, was the predestined cottage, half hidden by a thicket of fig trees, vines and laurels, sufficiently dense to serve as an oratory for St. Anne. The house itself consisted of one room, bright and spacious in front, but hewn from the dark rock in the rear. Fallen fortunes had reduced the descendants of the great Solomon to this pass; but by way of compensation, this was the place hallowed by the childhood of Mary and her happiest days."

Admittedly, Mary passed much of her girlhood in Nazareth, but this admission is not equivalent to saying that she was born there, nor does the symbolic comparison of her to a flower constitute enough evidence to identify a village with a name which means flower as her birthplace. Moreover, it was not unusual in those days, any more than it is now, to find that the country homes of well-to-do persons were much simpler and smaller than their city homes. But the opinion that Joachim was a poor man is certainly a minority one, as far as my research discloses. Indeed, one writer goes so far as to assert that:

"With his accumulated wealth, Joachim had been able to acquire, in addition to his flocks, a house in Nazareth and another in Jerusalem, without counting the one in Sephoris which came to him either by right of inheritance [It will be remembered that his father, Mathas, came from there] or through his marriage with Anne, who, according to tradition, was born there. According to Brother Lievan, he would have had a fourth house for his shepherds on Mt. Carmel, and St. Anne would have stayed there occasionally with the Virgin. In addition, according to certain Greek traditions, he possessed a country house near Jericho."[12]

All in all, the claims in favor of Jerusalem seemed based more on reason and substantiated fact, and less on sentiment and story than those in favor of Nazareth. Van der Vliet, in his carefully documented book, *Sainte Marie Où Elle Est Née Et La Piscine Probatique*, lists the following cogent reasons for his firm convictions on this score:

"Joachim had just offered a sacrifice and consulted the History of the Twelve Tribes. He is therefore at Jerusalem where the temple and the national archives are located. In leaving the temple, he did not go back to his wife. If she had not been at Jerusalem, this statement would have been superfluous.

"Anne, in her garden, is close to the 'fruitful waters,' near the vast reservoirs of the miraculous pool; her allusion explains itself. She has just said, 'I am not comparable to the brute animals, for even the brute animals are fruitful before thee, O Lord . . . I cannot be compared to *these* waters, for even the waters are fruitful before thee, O Lord.' Does she not seem to be designating the waters that are under her very eyes? Her expression is very significant.

"Joachim goes to his house in the evening, and *the next day* makes his offering at the temple; he, therefore, could not have been very far away from it. . . .

"On the occasion of Mary's first birthday, Joachim invited the priests and chief priests to his house. He, therefore, seems to have been at Jerusalem, for how can anyone reasonably suppose that he would have asked persons of such importance to take a three or four days' journey to celebrate the birthday of a year old child?

"Mary and Joachim ask, on the occasion of Mary's presentation at the temple, that the attendant virgins of Israel keep their lamps lighted, until they arrive there. If their house is close to the miraculous pool, this is easily understood; but the request is hard to comprehend if the family is living at a considerable distance from Jerusalem at that time."[13]

All the above conclusions are based on the text of the Protevangelium which, incidentally, is of much earlier origin—and therefore much closer to what was then current history—than the Gospel of the Birth of Mary. But Father Van der Vliet, with admirable fairness, remarks that, if this were the only source material available for determining Mary's birthplace, one would hesitate to accept it and mentions numerous others, among them the writings of St. John Damascene and St. Sophrone. The latter was a patriarch of the Holy City, and both refer in their writings to the birthplace of the Virgin there. Father Van der Vliet also notes that at the request of the Ordinary of the Church of St. Anne of Jerusalem, the votive masses of the Nativity of the Virgin and of the Immaculate Conception may be celebrated every day at the two altars in the crypt.

"Obviously, if the Holy See had claimed to settle this question, one could not do otherwise than accept its decision," he goes on to say. "But nothing is less accurate than the interpretation attributed to the Holy See of giving an official pronouncement on the subject of this topographical tradition. Julian II, speaking in a Brief of 1507, about the *Casa Santa* of Loretto, miraculously transported from Nazareth to Dalmatia, says that 'according to a pious belief' it is the room where

Mary was conceived and where she was brought up . . . where when she rose from earth to heaven, at the time of her Assumption, she fell asleep while praying.

"Other Bulls of Leo X (1519), Paul III (1535), Pius IV (1565), Sixtus V (1586), Innocent XII (1698) and Pius IX also mention the birth of the Holy Virgin at Nazareth. In the office of the translation of the *Casa Santa* at Loretto, it is said, in the sixth lesson, that this house is the birthplace of the Holy Virgin.

"Benedict XIV, one of the most learned Popes who has ascended the throne of St. Peter, indicates the rules which sovereign Pontiffs follow in questions of this kind, that is to say, simple historical facts, completely independent of dogma. Everything that has to do with the essence of doctrine, which the Popes wish to establish, must be received with complete respect. But they do not pretend to give to purely historical facts, which in no way affect either dogma or morals, any further value than that of the testimonials and proofs on which they can be based.

"Moreover, the Bull of Julian II does nothing more than recognize popular and pious legends which are, in effect, contradictory to history, but it does not change the nature of this and does not seek to approve it. We have seen the force of the proofs in favor of Jerusalem and nothing approaching these is claimed for Nazareth. It is also important to remember that the Bulls of the Popes following Julian II only repeat what he has said. . . . Moreover, there is no one now who would dare place the death and assumption of the Holy Virgin at Nazareth. The affirmation of her birth at Nazareth does not rest on any firmer ground. . . .

"Pope Urban IV is one of those most familiar with Oriental traditions, and especially those of Palestine, since, before being elected Pope, he was Patriarch of Jerusalem and Administrator of the Diocese of St. John of Acre in Galilee. It was during his Pontificate that a Sultan Bibars sacked Nazareth, and Urban reports that this sultan destroyed the Basilica of the Annunciation of Mary and the Incarnation of the World, which rendered this place worthy of the veneration of Christians. But he makes no allusion to the birth of the Blessed Virgin at Nazareth."

I could go on quoting, at much greater length, from Van der Vliet, for he has a veritable battery of arguments to support his claim, and I strongly recommend that anyone, deeply interested in the subject, read his valuable book; but to turn from this to Charland's, which seems to me equally valuable, let us quote the following passages:

"It is true that one may offer, as an objection [the claim for Jerusalem]—and the objection seems to be a serious one—the existence of certain Papal Bulls. One of the principal arguments of Monsignor Mislin [the mitred abbot of St. Mary of Deg in Hungary] rests primarily on the Bull of Julian II relative to the *Casa Santa* of Loretto, in which the birth of Mary at Nazareth is clearly supported. But, as one can see merely by reading it, this pontifical document does nothing more than establish popular and pious legends. The same may be said of the Bulls of Sixtus V, Innocent XIII and Pius IX, which only reproduce the text of that used by Julian II and have, historically, no other value.

"In the last analysis one may maintain, as Cardinal Lavigerie [to whom the French Government confided the care of the Church of St. Anne in Jerusalem in 1879] and Monsignor Mislin both say, that the Holy See has wished to cut short the historical discussion on the birthplace of Mary without contradicting itself, since on one hand it approves those who give Jerusalem as the birthplace of the Blessed Virgin and on the other approves those who give it as Nazareth. . . . One reconciles everything by saying, with Pope Benedict XIV, that the Popes have meant to leave to history all its prerogatives, in a question that is wholly historical, and that they have established, as factual, only the *existence* of the contradictory testimonials which have been submitted regarding Mary's birthplace. *Twenty Popes at least have caused to be inserted or attained, in the Roman breviary, the assertion of one of the most learned fathers of the Church—St. John Damascene—who affers that the Blessed Virgin was born in Jerusalem, and only five Popes have maintained that 'according to the popular belief of the populace she was born in Nazareth.'*"[14]

Personally, I should prefer to avoid all discussion of this debatable subject, which is what Rey, whom I so greatly admire, has done, or to remain neutral on it, like Charland, rather than to take a definite stand, like Van der Vliet. But since I am sure that I shall be asked for my opinion, it is, perhaps, better that I should give it now than later. All my own research, done both at home and abroad, all my travels in the Holy Land, both those undertaken recently and those undertaken long ago, all the conferences I have held with those who are in a position to know more about the subject than I do, incline me to feel that the arguments in favor of Jerusalem are the more convincing. This, as I have said before, is because they seem to have a firmer foundation than those in favor of Nazareth; and as far as the teachings of the Church are concerned, I can find nothing which does not leave me free to make this choice.

It is also my honest opinion that, whatever may be the conclusion elsewhere, the claim of Jerusalem is the one considered most convincing in the United States. On July 26, 1882, Bishop DeGoesbriand of Burlington, Vt. presented the Church of St. Anne in the nearby village of Milton with a 'relic of St. Anne in the shape of a stone which he had detached *from her home in Jerusalem* and brought from that place in 1880. On the same occasion, Miss Anne Quinn of Burlington gave a fine reliquary in which the relic is deposited.' That was seventy-five years ago and, as far as I am aware, no one has questioned the authenticity of this relic.

To bring forward a more recent example of my theory about American feeling, I may mention an item carried in *Catholic Action of the South* under date of June 3, 1954, in its illustrated feature, "Strange But True" by G. M. Murray, where an attractive little picture is captioned: "The figure of a tiny babe lies under the altar of the Grotto of the Nativity, site of Our Lady's birthplace, in St. Anne's Church, Jerusalem."

St. Anne Teaching the Virgin. Pinturicchio. Church of St. Onofrio, Rome.

VI

Though reliable sources differ, with such vehemence, regarding the place of the Virgin's birth, every one that I have consulted agrees that her presentation at the temple took place when she was three years old, and that she was educated there, with other young girls of her age and station in life. So, once again, let us quote from the two authors, who, in my opinion, tell the story most beautifully. Here is the version in the Gospel of the Birth of Mary:

"And when three years were expired, and the time of her weaning complete, they brought the Virgin to the temple of the Lord with offerings.

"And there were about the temple, according to the fifteen Psalms of degrees, fifteen stairs to ascend.

"For the temple being built in a mountain, the altar of burnt-offering, which was without, could not be come near but by stairs;

"The parents of the blessed Virgin and infant Mary put her upon one of these stairs;

Presentation at the Temple. F. Fiori detto il Baroccio. Church of St. Maria in Vallicella, Rome.

"But while they were putting off their clothes, in which they had travelled, and according to custom putting on some that were more neat and clean.

"In the mean time the Virgin of the Lord in such a manner went up all the stairs one after another, without the help of any to lead or lift her, that any one would have judged from hence that she was of perfect age.

"Thus the Lord did, in the infancy of his Virgin, work this extra-ordinary work, and the evidence by this miracle how great she was like to be hereafter.

"But the parents having offered up their sacrifice, according to the custom of the law, and perfected their vow, left the Virgin with other virgins in the apartments of the temple, who were to be brought up there, and they returned home."

And here is the version of the Protevangelium:

"And the child increased in strength every day, so that when she was nine months old, her mother put her upon the ground to try if she could stand; and when she had walked nine steps, she came again to her mother's lap.

"Then her mother caught her up, and said, As the Lord my God liveth, thou shalt not walk again on this earth till I bring thee into the temple of the Lord.

"Accordingly she made her chamber a holy place, and suffered nothing uncommon or unclean to come near her, but invited certain undefiled daughters of Israel, and they drew her aside.

"But when the child was a year old, Joachim made a great feast, and invited the priests, scribes, elders and all the people of Israel;

"And Joachim then made an offering of the girl to the chief priests, and they blessed her, saying, The God of our fathers bless this girl, and give her a name famous and lasting through all generations. And all the people replied, So be it, Amen.

"Then Joachim a second time offered her to the priest, and they blessed her, saying, O most high God, regard this girl, and bless her with an everlasting blessing.

Presentation of the Virgin at the Temple, Church of St. Séverin, Paris.

"Upon this her mother took her up, and gave her the breast, and sung the following song to the Lord.

"I will sing a new song unto the Lord my God, for he hath visited me, and taken away from me the reproach of mine enemies, and hath given me the fruit of his righteousness, that it may now be told the sons of Reuben, that Anna gives suck.

"Then she put the child to rest in the room which she had consecrated, and she went out and ministered to them.

"And when the feast was ended, they went away rejoicing and praising the God of Israel. . . . .

"But the girl grew, and when she was two years old, Joachim said to Anna, Let us lead her to the temple of the Lord, that we may perform our vow, which we have vowed unto the Lord God, lest he should be angry with us, and our offering be unacceptable.

"But Anna said, Let us wait the third year, lest she should be at a loss to know her father. And Joachim said, Let us then wait.

"And when the child was three years old, Joachim said, Let us invite the daughters of the Hebrews, who are undefiled, and let them take each a lamp, and let them be lighted, that the child may not turn back again, and her mind be set against the temple of the Lord.

Presentation at the Temple. Andrea Oroagna.
Church of St. Michele, Florence.

St. Anne Teaching the Virgin. Murillo.

"And they did thus till they ascended into the temple of the Lord. And the high-priest received her, and blessed her, and said, Mary, the Lord God hath magnified thy name to all generations, and to the very end of time by thee will the Lord shew his redemption to the children of Israel.

"And he placed her upon the third step of the altar, and the Lord gave unto her grace, and she danced with her feet, and all the house of Israel loved her."

At first glance, these charming stories of happy family life—including such delightful details as the age at which the Blessed Baby took her first steps, accounts of the party given on her first birthday and the beginning of her religious training, after her parents had thoughtfully and lovingly discussed these—would seem in contradiction with nearly every painting and statue representing her with her mother, prior to the birth of the Christ Child. Almost invariably, St. Anne is shown with a book in her hand, teaching her young daughter—and the young daughter appears to be at least ten years old, more often twelve or fourteen, if not in size—for this second figure is frequently very small—at least in face and form. Actually this is not as contradictory as one might think; the fact that the Virgin had been dedicated to the temple did not mean that she had been cloistered in it. Her father, who had an entree there, due to his father-in-law's official position, could certainly have seen her at any time; and her mother, universally recognized as a woman of culture and character, would very logically have been chosen to supplement the teachings of other instructors, as often as she was willing to do so. Moreover, there were periods that children and parents spent together, after school hours and in what then corresponded to "terms," just as there are now. What could be more natural than that during such periods a growing girl, an only daughter, should have turned to her mother for "help with her lessons" and that she should have received this fully and freely, to her lasting joy and benefit? It cannot be by accident that we have come to think of St. Anne as a great educator, no less than as a devoted wife, a dedicated mother, and a privileged grandmother.

St. Anne Teaching the Virgin. School of Murillo.

How great a part Joachim played in his daughter's education seems less certain. We know—if we accept as knowledge that part of our story which we have designated as silver treasure—that he was still living at the time of Mary's presentation at the temple, that his share in this ceremony was as important as his wife's; but after that he gradually disappears from the Chronicles, the statues and the paintings, though there are some which speak of him, or depict him, as present at Our Lady's marriage, and a few which record his presence in Nazareth when Mary and Joseph returned there after the Flight into Egypt. But while there are countless references to Anne as Our Lord's grand-mother, I have found few which refer to Joachim as His grandfather, and it therefore seems safe to assume that, at the very latest, he died soon after the birth of Christ.[15] We also find Anne and Mary increas-ingly associated with Nazareth, rather than with Jerusalem, which seems to suggest a loosening of logical ties with the latter place. And then we find, creeping into the Chronicles, the legend that Anne had three husbands.

Let us hasten to say that the Church no longer supports this legend, known as the Trinubium, though obviously it was countenanced at least, once upon a time, or so many representations of Anne with her triple family would never have been permitted. Let us also hasten to say that, even if the legend were true, there is nothing that seems in the least disparaging about it to the present writer, much less disgrace-ful, though admittedly some other modern writers have found it so. Personally, I feel the fact cannot be too often stressed that honorable wedlock was an integral part of Jewish life then, as it still is, and that no opprobium was attached to second or even third marriages, as long as they took place when the high contracting parties were widows or widowers—it was very different when divorce was involved. But I have my own reasons for regarding the legend as without firm foundation. In the first place, second and third marriages are, and always have been, very much less usual among widows whose lives are bound up in an only child, especially a child of great promise, than among child-less widows who have no such absorbing interest. In the second place, if St. Anne was nearly twenty when she was married—as we have every reason to believe that she was—and childless for twenty years more, she must have been nearly forty when Mary was born; and Joachim lived at least three years, probably more than that, after his daughter's birth, and it is quite possible that he lived that long after his Grandson's birth, which, of course, would completely nullify even consideration of the Trinubium. For the sake of argument, however, let us say that he lived until Mary was five years old, which seems a conservative estimate. His wife would then have been almost, if not quite, at the limit of normal

Central panel of triptich of carved, painted and gilded wood. Die Heilige Sippe. Franconian, circa 1500.

child-bearing age, and we are constantly reminded that Anne was, in every respect, a thoroughly normal woman. She had given up hope of a child, not because she was too old to have one, but because of the long continued fruitlessness. Since she was so sincerely attached to Joachim, her period of mourning would certainly have been long, less because this was proscribed than because it was instinctive. He had been the friend of her childhood, the only seriously considered suitor of her girlhood, the husband of her choice, the sharer of her sorrows and her joys for twenty years, and finally, the father of her child. The intimate associations of a lifetime are not easily put out of heart and mind by a woman of middle age.

It therefore seems to me unlikely, if not actually inconceivable, that Anne would have contemplated a second marriage within less than three years of Joachim's death, which would have brought her almost to the age of fifty; and though normal maternity is not unheard of at that age, it is very, very rare. As for maternity after fifty, that is, of course, rarer still. On these wholly commonplace grounds, if on no others, I decline to subscribe to the legend that Anne had three husbands. Nevertheless, since we are trying to present the stories about Anne as comprehensively as possible, and to illustrate these stories as graphically as known examples of art within our ken will permit, I think we should quote the best known version of the story.

This occurs in *The Golden Legend* of Jacques de Voragines and reads as follows:

"Anna is said to have had three husbands, namely, Joachim, Cleophas, and Salome. Of Joachim she begat one daughter, namely Mary the mother of the Lord, whom they gave in marriage to Joseph. At Joachim's death Anna became the wife of Cleophas, the brother of Joseph, and had of him another daughter, also called Mary, who was later given in marriage to Alpheus, and was the mother of four sons, namely James the Less, Joseph the Just (also called Barsabas), Simon, and Jude. When her second husband died, Anna took a third, namely Salome, of whom she had a third daughter, again called Mary, and given in marriage to Zebedee. This Mary bore two sons to Zebedee,

· 73 ·

namely James the Greater and John the Evangelist. All this is set forth in the following verse:

> *Anna solet dici tres concepisse Marias,*
> *Quas genuere viri Joachim, Cleophas, Salomeque.*
> *Has duxere viri Joseph, Alpheus, Zebedaeus.*
> *Prima parit Christum, Jacobum secunda minorem*
> *Et Joseph justum peperit cum Simone Judam,*
> *Tertia majorem Jacobum volucremque Joannem."*

Many persons have seized upon this fragmentary version of St. Anne's story in an endeavor to prove a close relationship between Jesus and certain of his disciples. Some of these persons are skeptics and scoffers, bent on undermining instinctive faith and readiness to accept the teachings of the Church, on the part of others. But it is only fair to add that some are sincere and devout non-Catholic Christians, who accept the Apostles' Creed as well as the Gospels in their entirety, and who never question the Dogma of the Virgin Birth, though they do question the doctrine of Our Lady's *perpetual* virginity, and believe that later she actually became the wife of Joseph, and bore several children of whom he was the father. Those of us who believe differently, however, and who feel we have a firm foundation for our belief, may be permitted to remind such persons, with courtesy and calmness, not only that the terms "cousins" and "brothers" were used interchangeably among the Hebrews to denote close relationship, just as "son" and "son-in-law," "daughter" and "daughter-in-law" are often found to be synonomous; but also, that we do not need the theory of the Trinubium to find cousins among Our Lord's relatives. It will be remembered that Joachim had a brother, Jacob, much younger than himself. Jacob was the father of a numerous family and it is also probable that he and Joachim had several sisters. The family chart, as presented by Émile Rey in his book, which has been officially approved by the Vatican and which is accepted unconditionally by the White

Fathers in charge of St. Anne's Sanctuary at Jerusalem, gives the various relationships as follows:

PARENTÉ DU CHRIST DANS LA TRIBU DE JUDA
avec dates de naissance approximatives.

MATHAN
dit Mathat (a)
descendant de David

HÉLIAKIM dit Joachim né en 57 avant J.-C. épouse Sainte Anne (de la tribu de Lévi)			JACOB né en 45 avant J.-C.	

MARIE née en 16 avant J.-C. épouse Saint Joseph	JOSEPH le Juste né en 20 avant J.-C. épouse la Vierge	JACQUES né en 15 avant J.-C. épouse la soeur de Cléophas	MARIE née en 10 avant J.-C. épouse Cléophas l'Alphée c.-à-d. le Sage	SALOMÉ née en 5 avant J.-C. épouse Zébédée

---

JESUS	JUDE dit Thaddée né en 8 après J.-C. Apôtre	JACQUES le mineur ou le petit né en 8 après J.-C. Apôtre	JOSEPH né en 10 après J.-C. (Non Apôtre)	SIMON le zélé ou le cananéen né en 12 après J.-C. Apôtre (c)	JUDE né en 14 après J.-C. (Non Apôtre)	JACQUES le majeur ou le grand né en 13 après J.-C. Apôtre	JEAN le bien-aimé né en 15 après J.-C. Apôtre (d)

If we, too, accept this table, as there seems to me no sound reason for declining to do, we will see that Our Lady had an uncle, namely Jacob, the younger brother of her father, Joachim; that Jacob's children, James, Mary and Salome, were her first cousins, as well as her brother-in-law and sisters-in-law; and that hence their children, all but one of whom became His apostles, were Our Lord's second cousins—a relationship which, in a patriarchal form of life, is already a very close one and which, in this instance, must have seemed even closer, because none of them was very much older than He was.

Let us therefore confidently proceed on the premise that Anne married but once, and that she lived long enough to enjoy her only grandchild, both in the way characteristic of all grandmothers, from the earliest ages to the present day, and with the added sense of responsibility and privilege which her instinctive knowledge that He was the Messiah must have given her. There is even reason to believe that she lived until after He was twelve years old, when He made the trip to Jerusalem with His parents, at the time of the Passover, which is so beautifully described in the Gospel of St. Luke,[16] and that when He left the "company," which was already on its way back to Nazareth, He went to His grandmother's house. Even if she spent most of her time in Nazareth by then, Anne would very logically have gone to Jerusalem, not only to take part in the Passover herself, but because it was very probably her Jubilee, in the sense that it was fifty years since her father's property had been turned over to her. If so, she would have been moved, both by natural inclination and by her respect for the ancient Law, to act in accordance with the commands set forth in Leviticus: "And thou shalt sanctify the fiftieth year . . . it is the year of jubilee. Every man shall return to his possession."[17]

Under these conditions, the first place that Mary and Joseph would have looked for Jesus would have been at Anne's home and she would have told them His whereabouts; this would have accounted for the fact that they did not go to the temple to find Him until the third day. In other words, they would have been reassured as to His safety and, not wishing to give Him the impression of being over-solicitous, they would have waited until the morning after their arrival to seek Him out, instead of doing so late in the evening, when they were tired after their long journey on foot and, moreover, when their presence in the temple might have seemed almost like an intrusion.

Personally, I find this theory very appealing. I like to think that the boy Jesus turned naturally to His grandmother's house, for I know how glad she would have been to have Him there with her—especially if she felt, as she must have done by then, that the times she could have Him with her were necessarily numbered, and that every one of these was doubly precious to her on that account.

SANTA ANA

In possession of author

St. Anne Teaching the Virgin.
Porcelain tile. Portuguese.

The Virgin and St. Anne. Lorenzo de Sanseverino.

VII

As I have said before, St. Anne's story, which seemed to me such a simple one before I started to write it, proved impossible to tell without the interruption of several different versions—some because they were worthy of serious consideration and some because they required refutation. It has also proved impossible, at least for this writer, to tell the story by following, in chronological order, the events which make it important as well as absorbing. For example, having reached the account of the presentation at the temple, it was essential to stop and consider how long thereafter Joachim probably lived, because this had a definite bearing on Anne's later life: whether she married again, and how long she herself lived and where and how. Now, having reached the conclusion, after the most careful thought and the most careful research possible, that she married only once and that she lived to a ripe old age, we must return to the point where, having offered her only child to the temple at the age of three, Anne was still taking an active part in the education of that child while Mary was a growing girl. Since this return *is* necessary, in order to tell Anne's story as fully as possible, I hope it will not make the text seem involved and, therefore, confusing to the average reader. After all, the procedure I am following is nothing more or less than the flashback technique so greatly in vogue at present; it is the development of an old, old tale in an ultramodern way. Let us try to accept it as such!

It was customary that the young girls who were being educated at the temple should remain there until they were of marriageable age and that they should then return to their parents' homes. This, after all, differed very little from the current custom in many respects; young girls who are today being educated at boarding schools, whether their teachers are nuns or laywomen, usually remain there until they are grown up. The main difference of which we need to be mindful lies in the fact that, in the Orient, the age of puberty is usually earlier than in the Occident, and always has been. Girls like Mary and her companions would, therefore, have been as fully developed at fourteen or sixteen as the average English and American girls of eighteen or twenty. A minor but also important difference, lies in the fact that we no longer take it for granted that every girl will wish to get married, and that her parents will wish to have her do so, as soon as she finishes school. Much less, if she failed to do so, would she also be failing not only to comply with custom but with ancient law, nor would her choice, if she made one, be circumscribed by other ancient laws.

Bearing all this in mind, we read, with understanding interest, of the high priest's order "that all virgins who had public settlements in the temple, and were come to this age [fourteen] should return home and, as they were now of proper maturity, should, according to the custom of their country, endeavor to be married." Also that accordingly, "The virgin of the Lord, Mary, with seven other virgins of the same age, who had been weaned at the same time, and who had been appointed to attend her by the priest, return to her parents' house in Galilee."

Now that their daughter could be with them until her marriage, it was logical that Anne and Joachim[18] should wish to divide their time between Jerusalem and Nazareth, instead of spending most of it in Jerusalem, as they had while she was at the temple. Their joint inheritances—Anne's in Jerusalem, Joachim's in Nazareth—were equally important to them, and they were responsible for safeguarding these, not only on their own account, but on their child's. To be sure, Joachim's younger brother, Jacob, had faithfully watched over the former's interests all these years; but his chosen occupation was that of a carpenter, and his eldest son, Joseph, had now followed him in this trade—a quiet, industrious, self-effacing young man, rather reserved in his attitude toward the opposite sex, who had early been designated as "the Just" because of his outstanding rectitude. It was natural that Jacob should wish to devote more and more time to his partnership with this son, and that Joachim should feel it fair to make this possible.

It was to Nazareth that Mary went then, after she had finished her studies at the temple and was of marriageable age; and it is easy to picture Anne's joy in having this beloved child with her again. It is also easy to picture her first bewilderment and concern on learning that Mary preferred to order her life in much the same devout way that she had at the temple, rather than to take advantage of her freedom from its restrictions in the pursuit of pleasure, and that the prospect of marriage did not appeal to her. It must have been much the same feeling that an elderly woman has nowadays when an only daughter, born when her mother had given up hopes of maternity, reveals, with some hesitation and becoming respect, but nevertheless with firmness, her desire to return, as a nun, to the convent where she has been educated, and not to raise a family of her own!

We know what would happen, in our own day and age, if such an elderly woman were also calm, cultured and herself naturally devout: she would tell her daughter that a decision like this could not be taken hastily—it was too important, too far reaching in its consequences; they must think it over, prayerfully, by themselves, and they must talk it over, quietly, together. I believe this is exactly what Anne would have done—what she did do. Then she would almost certainly go on to say that Mary, of course, remembered the ancient law about marriageable maidens and, finally, she would bring forth the most telling argument of all—that the time was ripe for the coming of the Messiah, that to be His mother would be the greatest privilege which could ever come to any woman, and that Mary, because of her descent from David, was among those who might hope for this signal honor. Having said all this, and having found that it made no difference in her daughter's viewpoint, she would have gone to talk the matter over with her husband and he would have suggested a simple and sensible solution.

We have been given, of course, a much more sensational account of this part of the story: that Mary had already confided in the high priest before she left the temple, and that he had taken alarm, and had sent out a summons to all bachelors and widowers in the region, requiring them to present themselves promptly as suitors; that he asked heaven for a sign, in the form of a blossoming rod or an encircling dove, in the hand or around the head of the one who was most worthy—who proved to be Joseph. This account has gained credence through the depiction of great painters, as well as through the chronicles of devout scribes. But, as usual, it is a version of the story founded on logic rather than

The Betrothal of the Virgin. Church of St. Séverin, Paris.

on fantasy that I prefer to present as probably the more factual: Joachim, upon being presented with the problem in question by his troubled wife, reminded her that his eldest nephew, Joseph, the son of the faithful Jacob, was his natural heir since he and Anne had no son of their own; that the tribal laws regarding marriage were fulfilled in Joseph, and the promise of the Messiah safeguarded; that he and Mary had long known and loved each other as cousins[19] and that they both might very easily be persuaded that this affection should take a different turn. If they agreed, well and good; if not, then it would be time enough to think what should be done next.

As so often happens, the simplest thing, the most natural thing, was also the wisest thing. Neither Joseph nor Mary made the slightest objection to an early bethrothal. Since Joseph was such a model of rectitude, since Mary was incapable of dissimulation, it is inconceivable that, in talking privately together, they should not have been completely candid with each other about the nature of their prospective alliance; but as far as their little world was concerned, there was nothing unusual, much less anything extraordinary about it. Their betrothal took place with the usual witnesses and the usual solemnity of celebration; it was regarded as binding as the marriage ceremony which would take place a year later. But meanwhile, still in accordance with established custom, Mary remained in her parents' house.

And then came the great miracle of the Incarnation.

Collection of the Duchess of Parcent

The Betrothal of the Virgin. Wood carving.

The Annunciation. Bronzino. St. Anne's Cathedral, Apt.

VIII

To learn about this, to be reminded of it, we do not need the chronicle of any writer who—however learned, however devout—has been declared Apocryphal in the considered judgment of those to whom was left the final decision as to what should be included in Holy Scripture or excluded therefrom. St. Luke has given it to us in magnificent form;[20] and in one form or another we recall it constantly ourselves. Assuredly then, every reader will understand the present writer's reluctance to do more than refer to it, and that with awe and reverence. The feeling that a fresh account, or even more than such a reference, would be both superfluous and presumptuous, already so strong in regard to certain previous scenes and episodes, is now intensified a hundredfold. But St. Luke was telling us about the effect of the angel's visit *on Mary*, and it is this we, ourselves, have in mind when we recite the *Credo* or the *Ave Maria*; St. Luke did not tell us anything about the effect of the angel's visit on Mary's mother, nor do we have this in mind when we bear witness to our faith or make our daily petitions.

So perhaps I may venture to say something about that. After all, it is St. Anne's story I am trying to tell, and Gabriel's visit marked a great moment in her life, too.

I believe that her reactions were not unlike her daughter's; first must have come incredulity, then wonderment, then submission. The incredulity would have been fleeting; who could know better than Anne, from her own experience, that with God all things are possible? She would have continued to marvel somewhat longer, but there would have been no unbelief in her wonderment. And the submission would have been shot through with gladness, for with it would have come the sure conviction that the promised child, conceived by the Holy Ghost, would be the long expected Messiah, that Mary would be His mother and she and her husband His grandparents. Suddenly she would have recalled the words of the prophet, Isaias, which, from her youth, she had heard repeated again and again: "Therefore the Lord himself shall give you a sign. Behold a virgin shall conceive and bear a son: and his name shall be called Emmanuel"[21]; also, the words of the angel who had appeared to her before Mary's birth, promising her not only that she would have a daughter, but that this daughter would be "blessed above all women" and that, as a virgin, she would bring forth a son "who . . . both by His grace and name and works shall be the Saviour of the world." With these recollections would have come the certainty that her daughter was the predestined virgin of whom the prophet and the angel spoke and she would hasten to tell the good tidings of great joy to Joachim.

He may be forgiven if he received these with feelings of more tempered happiness. Not that he would have been unfamiliar with ancient Scripture, or that he would have doubted the promise of the prophet and the angel. Not that he would have disbelieved the story of Gabriel's visit. Not that he would have failed to feel the imminence of the Messiah's coming and the glory of it. But I think he would also have felt a human father's natural concern for his daughter—concern, which, in the case of his wife, had been submerged in exaltation. Mary was still living at home, solemnly betrothed to Joseph, but still not officially married to him. It was not regarded as irregular for a betrothed couple

Altarpiece from the Church of St. Anne in Granada, showing St. Anne and St. Joachim in adoration of the Virgin.

to come together as husband and wife; indeed, such a union was considered wholly legal, and its offspring, if acknowledged by the husband, was of unquestioned legitimacy. On the other hand, such prenuptial intimacy was not in accordance with the strict usages of good society. It would, of course, be necessary for Joseph to make an immediate statement to the effect that Mary's father and mother had already accepted him as their son-in-law.[22] Joachim would have a talk with Jacob, which should assure family solidarity on the subject. And perhaps Anne had better talk to Jacob's wife. . . .

Legend has been singularly silent on the subject of the latter woman, whose very name is unrecorded; even those who have based their telling of Anne's story on their visions, like the Spanish nun, Maria Agreda, have not, as far as I am aware, professed to know anything about Jacob's wife. Certainly I would not venture any such profession. Nevertheless, as a deeply interested friend has reminded me, it would be fascinating to speculate about her; and ever since this suggestion was made to me, I have been unable to refrain from doing so. The public declaration so promptly made by Joseph would, of course, have relieved her mind to a certain extent; she would not have known that Joseph, too, had been having his troubled moments, and that, much as he loved Mary, his mind had not been entirely at rest until he had been reassured and enlightened by a dream of Divine origin. His mother would probably have been displeased with her eldest son and disappointed in him; and she would have had hard work to refrain from thinking and saying that Mary, who had had far greater cultural advantages than he had had, and who should, therefore, have been more mindful of the proprieties, should have insisted on a strict observance of them, whatever Joseph's attitude might have been. She would almost certainly have been skeptical about the angelic visit; and when reminded that Joachim and Anne had had similar experiences, she might well have replied, rather drily, that they had already been married twenty years when these took place, if indeed there had actually been visitations rather than visions. As for Isaias' prophecy, that had been made centuries before, and many of the prophets' sayings had been handed down by word of mouth, from generation to generation; it was

easy enough to make changes in them, either advertently or inadvert-
ently, to suit a singer's tastes or to raise false hopes in times of trouble.
Having said all this she might next announce that her watchful care
of her own little daughters, Mary and Salome, would become more
zealous than ever before. Then gradually, her attitude would have
changed, as she saw that Anne was not only calm, but joyous, in the
face of coming events, and as she found that Mary was all she could
have hoped for, and far, far more, in her son's wife. She would have
blamed herself for blaming him and his bride and she would have let
Anne see that she realized the error of her ways and would have con-
fessed that she, too, was looking forward to the baby's birth with eager
anticipation.

All this, of course, is mere speculation. What we do know, as a certainty, is that Mary quietly solved the problem of whether she should
continue to live in her parents' home or that of her parents-in-law by
expressing the wish to visit her cousin, Elizabeth. There was a great
difference in the ages of the two; it will be remembered that Anne was
only eight years old when her sister, Hismarian, married, and that Hismarian's baby, Elizabeth, was born shortly thereafter, whereas Anne
had been married twenty years before the birth of Mary; and though
Elizabeth, after her marriage to Zacharias, lived at Ain Kerem, only a
few miles from Jerusalem, the fact that Mary was brought up in the
temple would have precluded much visiting on her part. Probably she
did not care to do any, especially as these kinfolk would have been free
to visit her, since Zacharias was a priest "of the course of Abia," whose
"lot was to burn incense when he went to the temple of the Lord." Her
life was full and complete, and when she left the temple for Nazareth,
she had the companionship of other cousins near her own age, Joseph
among them. But now she was aware of a new kinship with Elizabeth:
they were both expecting children under circumstances which were
miraculous, Elizebeth because of her great age, Mary because of the
Incarnation. They would have much to say to each other, much to
learn from each other, because of these great mysteries, which they
could share with no one else so well.

I doubt if Mary would have needed to stress this point. Anne and

Joachim and Joseph would all have understood it; Jacob and his wife would have accepted it.

The journey to Jerusalem was a long one, and it was, of course, unthinkable that Mary should undertake it alone, in her condition. But it was logical, or could be made to seem so, that her parents should go with her. To be sure, it was not long since they had left their city home, and the supervision of their property was in good hands; but then, it had always been understood that they were to go back and forth between their two places. This was as good a time as any for a journey.

It was, in fact, an excellent time. Spring is very beautiful in Palestine. The cruel cold of winter has gone, the cruel heat of summer has not come. The fields are covered with brilliant wildflowers—those "lilies of the field" with which Solomon's glory could not compare, as Mary's Son was later to remind certain of His listeners, who were troubled about trifles. The skies were very blue by day, the stars very close by night. The travellers took the journey in easy stages, and Mary rested at her childhood home, before she went on the last short lap of her journey alone.

Her parents would have been glad to accompany her still further, and when she urged them not to make the additional effort, which seemed to her unnecessary, they besought her to take one of their faithful servants with her. They could not help feeling concerned at the thought of leaving her unaccompanied; after all, she was their cherished only daughter and she was still a young girl; moreover, she was with child. They were loath to have her go alone. But, for some reason, she felt that was the way it must be, and they did not insist.

She must have looked very lovely as she started out, her blue veil framing her pure face and floating out behind her. Did Anne and Joachim know, as they watched her walking down the road, carrying herself with characteristic ease and grace, that to all intents and purposes she was leaving them forever? I think they must have, and that it must have been very hard for them to see her go. I think they realized that when her visit to Elizabeth was ended, and father and mother and daughter went back to Nazareth together, Mary must go to her husband's house to take the place expected of her as his wife—a place

The Flight into Egypt. Church of St. Séverin, Paris.

which would require her, later on, to go to Bethlehem with him to be taxed, not in the beautiful mild spring, but in the harsh winter. That time it would have been harder still to see her go—so hard that the ordeal would have put a great strain on Joachim's waning strength, the anxiety caused by the Flight into Egypt a still greater one—more than he could endure. He died, as he had lived, with dignity, and was buried in the tomb of his fathers, a hillside tomb hewn from the solid rock and sealed, when the services were over, by a great stone.

The mourners withdrew, the pipes were silenced. Anne went back to her home, facing years of widowhood which would have been very lonely for her, if she had not been a grandmother. For now we have come back to the place where I said, "I like to think that the boy Jesus turned naturally to His grandmother's house, for I know how glad she would have been to have Him there with her—especially if she felt, as she must have done by then, that the times she could have Him with her were necessarily numbered, and that every one of these was doubly precious to her on that account."

The Virgin and Child with St. Anne. Leonardo and pupils.

Madonna and Child with St. Anne. Bernardino Luini.

IX

The house was very quiet except when the Boy was there, but Anne liked it that way. It did not seem sad to her to have a quiet house, only restful, and she seemed to need a great deal more rest nowadays than she had when she was younger. She went to bed earlier at night and rose later in the morning than had formerly been her habit, but still she found she was glad of a chance to rest in the afternoon, too. She kept busy through the early part of the day, spinning and stitching and supervising the housework; but during the latter part of it she liked to sit in her garden, under the shade of the old laurel tree,[23] a copy of the Scriptures within easy reach. It was pleasant and peaceful to sit there, reading from time to time, or merely resting some more.

She still answered every call upon her from the sick and suffering in as far as her strength would permit, and often when it did not. But she went back and forth between Nazareth and Jerusalem less and less. The journey tired her. Besides, she preferred to have her family visit her rather than to visit them, and it was simpler to bring this about if she remained in Jerusalem: since none of the others had houses there, it was obvious that they should visit her. Besides, as long as she was in her old home, there never need to be a possibility that any of them would have to stay at an inn, or be turned away from one. It was still hard for Anne to think, with resignation, of what had happened at Bethlehem, though she tried to do so. She told herself that perhaps the shepherds would not have found Mary and Joseph and "the Babe lying in a manger" so easily if they had been at the inn. And this visit had meant a great deal to the shepherds, there could be no doubt of that— perhaps more than anything that had ever happened to them before or ever would again. She tried not to think harshly of that innkeeper who had turned away her daughter, in Mary's hour of need.

But there was very little on which her thoughts dwelt that required an effort of charity on her part. Her pleasant childhood—her happy

St. Anne with the child Jesus. Convent entrance, Malaga. (This is the only representation we have found of St. Anne alone with the Child.)

marriage—her triumphant maternity—the great gift of her Grandson—as she sat under the laurel tree with folded hands, looking back on these, she could indeed feel that goodness and mercy had followed her all the days of her life. And she did. Nor could she doubt that she would dwell in the House of the Lord forever.

She was not as wealthy as she had been in her husband's lifetime. Some of her property had passed out of her hands. It did not matter, except that she had less to share with the poor, and that troubled her. But what did she need of extra houses any more? It had tired her to take care of them, and she had not been to any of them, except the one in Nazareth, for a long while. As a matter of fact, of course she did not need that one, either—she could always stay at her daughter's, where she was very welcome. But she loved staying at home, in Jerusalem. Just like this.

The flocks had gradually been reduced in size, too. Her son-in-law, Joseph, like his father Jacob before him, had always preferred to ply his trade of carpenter in a town, rather than to spend it in pastoral pursuits. She thought her Grandson did, too, though He was very familiar with every aspect of the countryside and loved it all. Probably, when He got older, He would spend more time in it; it was inconceivable, with His heritage, that He should not have something of the shepherd in Him and, if so, this would be apparent, in one way or another. But there was no use in worrying about an inheritance for Him, since He was utterly indifferent to money and to personal possessions of any kind. Indeed, it would not surprise her if He gave most of His away to those needier than Himself, once He had provided for His mother, in case His foster father died first. That would be contrary to custom, but this did not matter, either. Someone must start new customs, the old ones were becoming outworn; and Who better than Jesus? What a promising Boy He was! How well He knew the Scriptures! How brilliantly He had talked in the temple! And He had the physical vigor to match His mental alertness and His spiritual strength. He would never be content to go on, all His life, plying a small trade in a small town. He would have a great career, an inspired career. He was indeed the prophesied Messiah; He would indeed deliver His people. How and when, He would know in His own good time. There had never been such a Boy, there never would be again! Of course, other women thought that about their grandsons, too. But Anne did not *think* this. She knew it.

Probably she would not live to see Jesus accomplish all His great ends. But that was something else which did not matter very much, since she was so sure it would happen. She could let her thoughts dwell on the future with confidence, just as they dwelt on the past with joy.

She thought of her own mother these days more than she had in a long while. It pleased her to remember that her birth had been a source of happiness, not as great, of course, as her daughter's had been to her, but still very great. She had been slow to recall—perhaps slow to believe—her mother's story of visiting a holy hermit who told her that she would never have a son, but that she would have a daughter who, in turn, would give birth to a "most holy virgin, even the future mother of God." She had thought of this, of course, when the angel had appeared to Mary; but she had not mentioned it, even to Joachim, for fear it would seem as if she were trying to compare a humble, obscure hermit with the great Isaias, in gifts of prophecy, or subject her mother to the suspicion of having hallucinations. Now she allowed her thoughts to dwell on the visit to the hermit and his words more freely, though she still did not speak of them. Indeed, there was no one to whom she wished to speak of them. She was a very old woman now; she had outlived most of her girlhood friends; and though she had had a wide acquaintance, as a matron, few persons had been her intimates. She had not felt the need of confidantes, outside her harmonious and understanding family circle. She did not feel the need of them now. . . .

There was something else her mother had told her that she had not thought much about when she was younger, that she had not wholly believed. This was the story about the golden letters which had appeared mysteriously, perhaps miraculously, in her mother's room, over and over again: the letters which spelled out her own name, A-N-N-A, the meaning of which was grace. Well, it would do no harm to believe the story now. Why not? Certainly she believed in the grace of God. He had shared it in abundance with her daughter—"Hail, Mary, *Full of Grace*, the Lord is with Thee." Those were the words with which the angel's salutation had begun. If God had been willing to share some small portion of His great grace with her, too, should she not be grateful rather than doubtful?

It was a happy thought to take with her as she drifted off into dreams and finally, into the peaceful, prayerful sleep from which there was no waking. . . .

This is the way I believe it all was. Of course, I cannot be sure. But there is one thing of which I am sure; and this is that never could Anne have dreamed that two thousand years later her name would still be written in letters of gold in the Calendar of Saints.

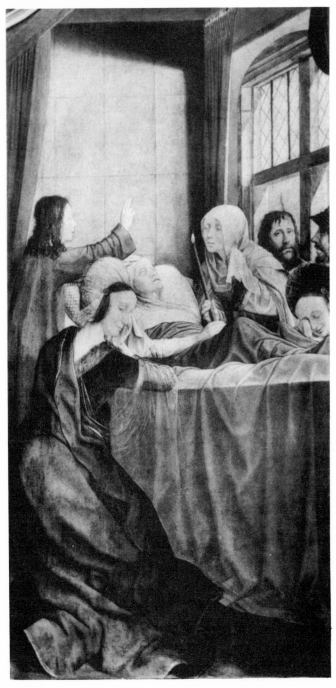

Royal Museum of Fine Arts. Brussels

The Death of St. Anne. Quentin Matsys.

X

Though an unmarried woman is buried beside her parents, it is usual today for a widow to be buried in the same place where her husband has previously been laid to rest, whether this place is a magnificent mausoleum or a simple family lot in a country cemetery. There is nothing about this custom which surprises us; it seems fitting that in death, as in life, man and wife should remain united. Therefore, neither should it surprise us to learn—if we did not know it already—that this custom goes back a long way, in both time and space. We can easily take it for granted that St. Anne was buried in her husband's ancestral tomb, with the same ceremonial of mourners and music that had characterized his funeral. What is less easy to take for granted is the fact that this was not her last resting place, for many of us instinctively shrink from the very thought of disturbing the dead. It is on this point that we need to put ourselves in the position of the early followers of Jesus Christ.

Heartrending as it is to recall, we should bring ourselves to remember that the first Christians celebrated Mass on the mutilated bodies of the martyrs. Soon the possession of their saints' mortal remains became an obsession, almost a matter of jealous rivalry among them, for only through such possession could reverent burial be assured and hallowed tombs protected. Moreover, these early believers could not bring themselves to face complete separation from the mortal remains which they safeguarded and which were sacred to them. The least part of these was cherished and reverenced; and it was in order that these parts might be shared, that no one person and no one group should be privileged above any other, that removals from original sepulchres and divisions of what had been there entombed became more and more general. These were not acts of desecration; they were acts of veneration; and since the number of Christian believers increased very rapidly, and the Apostles took very literally their Master's command that they should go out into all the world and teach the gospel to all people, it was natural that they should take with them, when they went, what they held most sacred and most dear—namely, the relics of their saints.[24]

These conversions and these apostolates certainly began almost immediately after the coming of the Holy Ghost—that is to say, after the first Pentecost.[25] Though it is less certain, it is highly probable, that among the first of the voluntary missionary exiles were Lazarus of Bethany and his sisters, Mary Magdalene and Martha. They had the private means which would permit them to undertake an extended journey without being a burden to anyone, and it is unthinkable that there could have been any other purpose to which they would so eagerly have put their wealth. Moreover, they may well have had humanly selfish reasons for being glad to leave Palestine: Lazarus was the object of especial suspicion and hostility on the part of the Sanhedrin, who had no belief in immortality, and to whom the very thought of a miracle whereby a dead man had been resurrected was anathema. They were almost equally skeptical and scathing on the subject of Mary Magdalene's repentence; certainly they could have made life very unpleasant, if not actually dangerous, for this brother and sister. The second sister, Martha, would have been more troubled than ever over many things if she had thought the others were in peril. It was natural that Maximin, a cousin of this trio, should be glad to accompany them; it is a little less clear why Mary Jacobe and Mary Salome should have been selected to form a part of this particular company; but it is probably because, as cousins of Jesus, they had become acquainted with His personal friends and fond of them. Their inclusion in the group of missionaries certainly had a very marked effect upon its character, for, besides being the cousins of Jesus, they were the nieces of Anne; in leaving their native land, they evidently felt that they could not bear to be eternally separated from all tangible contact with their blood relations, especially since this contact was also their closest link with their acknowledged Saviour. Jesus' mother, who kept so many things in her heart, must have understood this; certainly it was with her willing consent that, when Mary Jacobe and Mary Salome left Nazareth for good, they took with them a coffer, fashioned from cedar wood, containing the relics they so ardently desired to possess and to transport to their new home.[26]

The Glorification of St. Anne. J. B. Francken.

Evidently the boat on which these missionaries travelled carried many others as well, and stopped at numerous ports along the way, to permit disembarkation of passengers for several other points, before it finally reached Massilia, which we know as Marseilles. Then, as now, it was a great commercial city, superbly located; its harbor and its surrounding countryside must have looked very beautiful to the weary pilgrims; and evidently the group in which we are especially interested was warmly welcomed by those Jews who themselves had made a Pentecostal pilgrimage to Jerusalem, who had there been converted to Christianity, and who already knew the voluntary exiles, either personally or by reputation; indeed, we may assume that they had been partially responsible for the destination of the others. The mechanics of the new apostolate were promptly put into operation: Lazarus became the first Bishop of Marseilles; Mary Magdalene, who later withdrew into strict seclusion at Sainte Baume, remained with her brother long enough to help him in the organization of his mission, thus following the custom, general among early converts, whereby men and women who were blood relations complemented each other's work. Maximin pushed further inland to the little city of Apt, which nestles among the mountains, and Martha, in accordance with the same custom, accompanied him. The two Marys transshipped to a smaller vessel, and took up their abode in a wild, marshy region, where their work would be largely among humble fisherfolk.[27] It was the way of life which they deliberately chose, well aware of the primitive conditions under which they must labor and the hardships they must endure. But they did not feel it could provide a suitable shrine for their precious relic. They, therefore, entrusted this to the safe-keeping of Lazarus, hoping only to visit it from time to time, as needed intervals of rest permitted.

The Apostolate of Lazarus was long and fruitful; when he died, the mission he had founded was prosperous and seemed secure. But eventually, Massilia, like Jerusalem before it, became the scene of repeated invasion and siege. In time, a successor of Lazarus decided that the relic of St. Anne was no longer safe in his keeping; he took counsel with other churchmen, and it was decided that the Bishopric of Apt, founded by Maximin, should have the honor of protecting it.

It was still encased, quite simply, in the coffer made from cedar in which it had been brought from Palestine; now it seemed wiser to inclose this coffer in another, more substantial, and to put both under lock and key. Eventually, even this did not seem safe enough, either; it was decided that the coffers must be concealed altogether, and that their hiding place must be so complete that this would never be discovered until the time was ripe. The question of how to bring about this concealment presented a grave problem. Again there was a council of great minds.

From this council came a second decision: the coffers should be placed in an opening of the wall excavated from a subterranean gallery known as the *Antrum Antiquum,* which had originally been a branch of the catacombs. It was reached by a short flight of steps and hedged in by the cathedral ramparts. This wall opening, which would now become an ossuary, would be sealed in and not marked in any way; but on that part of the passage ceiling which was directly beside it a design would be carved, intelligible only to the initiate.

This design is still visible, in exactly the same form wherein it was graven so many centuries ago. It consists of the flowering branch of a tree, interlaced with a vine bearing both foliage and grapes. To look at it is an experience so moving that, months after gazing at it, this chronicler finds it impossible even to write of it without profound emotion. For it reveals, unmistakably, that when the stone slab was carved, even as now, men and women were reverently reciting the litany which begins:

"St. Anne, Grandmother of our Saviour, pray for us."

And continues:

"St. Anne, Root of Jesse,

St. Anne, Fruitful Vine . . . pray for us."

Personally, we require no further confirmation of our belief that this became St. Anne's last resting place. But the doubting Thomas—or Thomasine, as the case may be—has only to look at the slab beside the one which shows the root of Jesse and the fruitful vine. On this second slab appears these words:

Antulfus, Alif, Anselmus, Alboinus, Berardus, sac. vel cl.

Émile Rey interprets the Latin abbreviation as meaning. *Sacerdotes vel clavicularii*—priests and guardians—giving as his reason for doing so, that this interpretation seems "the one that is most natural and that most closely conforms to history." On the other hand, the learned antiquarian, Joseph-Marie de Suarez, Bishop of Vaison, in the 17th Century, believed them to be abbreviations for *Sancti Veli Clavicularii* —Guardians of the Holy Veil—namely those in charge of the relics, which were wrapped in a winding sheet, or holy veil. Either interpretation seems admissible, in view of later records. But this author agrees with Émile Rey that the former is more natural and, therefore, has used it in continuing her story. For she also agrees with him that "this is the official seal of the relics of St. Anne."

Ceiling of the interior crypt, Cathedral of St. Anne, Apt. (Symbolic sculpture by means of which the tomb of St. Anne was discovered.)

XI

The "priests and guardians" designated on the slab marking St. Anne's tomb have been identified, by historians more learned than this one can ever hope to be, as having lived in Apt during the 6th century. They had acted none too soon in hiding their precious treasure. In 576 A.D. this city was badly damaged by an invading army of the Lombards and its surviving inhabitants, both lay and clerical, were scattered far and wide. After a century of desolation, another invasion took place, this time at the hands of the Saracens. But somehow, a few pious persons must have guarded the secret of the hidden tomb with the utmost caution, handing down their knowledge of it from one generation to another; for it cannot be wholly by accident that this hiding place was finally discovered in a great and glorious way, by a great and glorious person—none other than Charlemagne himself.

We are told by Kleinclausz, his brilliant contemporary biographer, that he "visits all the most famous sanctuaries: St. Martin of Tours, St. Peter's of Rome, which is particularly dear to him and where he has been four times to pray; he also assists at the transfer of sacred remains from one place to another and at the dedication of churches where they are enshrined. These relics are the object of special attention on his part, for 'though they now disintegrate in dust, they will revive full of glory at the end of the world and reign eternally with Christ.' He causes them to be searched for at Rome, Constantinople and Jerusalem and, when found, shares them with his friends."

"Is it possible," Émile Rey inquires, after thus quoting from Kleinclausz and Charlemagne himself, "that a monarch so learned, so far-seeing, so powerful, could ignore St. Anne? Hagiography replies 'no!' That is why the Carolingian litanies, composed during the Pontificate of Hadrian I, and in constant use at the palace in Aix-le-Chapelle contain the name of St. Anne, whereas all other names (except for rare exceptions and for some special reason) were those of French saints.

One sees with what veneration Charlemagne regarded the mother of the Holy Virgin. He was well informed regarding the Aptian tradition, faithfully handed down, as we have said, by priests and guardians. That is why, a little later, he caused a search to be made for these relics, and why he insisted, on this occasion, in passing through Apt.[28]

"At what time and under what circumstances? On this point, history is positive. This pilgrimage could have been undertaken only after the coronation at Rome of the king who had become an emperor.[29] And it is the only journey he would have made in Provence. 'He spent the entire winter in Rome,' Kleinclausz tells us, 'then, having celebrated Easter there on April 4th, 801, he felt the time to leave had arrived and, three weeks later, took the road to Spoleto. He was still there on the 30th, when a violent earthquake caused a large part of St. Peter's roof to collapse. From Spoleto he went to Ravenna, where he spent several days, then traversed Bolognese territory and, by way of Padua . . . reached the Alps.' From there, he crossed through the Pass of Cenis to Maurienne. Then, by way of Embrun, Sisteron, Forcalquier, Cereste and Rustrel, following the direction of the *Via Domitia,* he arrived in Apt around July 23, 801."

It has been significantly said that "Rome, which gave Provence its name, has left there ruins worthy of the power which refused no one a share in its grandeur because it had enough for the whole world."[30] Truly, it is only those whose own splendor is a sham who need to be niggardly with it, just as it is only those whose own social position is doubtful who are condescending or overbearing in their attitude toward their fellow men. Apt had been a free city under the Romans, and still retained many evidences of that "shared grandeur": an imposing amphitheater, massive walls, lofty towers, wide gates. To these had been gradually added the noble and distinctive art and architecture of the early Christian Era; and though the latter embellishments, like the Roman relics, had suffered during the invasions of the Lombards and the Saracens, a degree of recovery had taken place, before the ninth century, sufficient to restore to the little city much of its proud estate; and the natural beauty of its location, in a verdant valley surrounded by rocky peaks and watered by sparkling cascades, gave it the added advantage of a fine setting. It was both a bishopric and an earldom and, between them, its bishop and its count governed it effectively, impartially dividing the duties of church and state.

It was these two functionaries, with their respective suites, who went forth to meet Charlemagne on the *Via Domitia* and officially bid him welcome to their city. The spectacle must have been a magnificent one. Charlemagne was in the prime of life, a splendid specimen of vitality and vigor. He sat his superb charger with accomplished ease, handling the reins with a dexterity which concealed all evidence of curbing. He held his fine head high and his strong body erect. His abundant hair was auburn, his face ruddy, his eyes piercingly blue; and if his very presence bespoke authority, it was an authority tempered by a strong sense of justice, instinctive piety and natural geniality. Though by preference plain as to dress, he was garbed in the sumptuous manner befitting this great occasion; his brilliant escort of 3,000 was headed by outstanding dignitaries, clerical, military and civil; he could not permit them to outdo him in proud array.

As soon as the first formalities of welcome were over, the entire cortege proceeded direct to the cathedral, where a *Te Deum* was sung. Almost immediately thereafter, the emperor, who had been looking about him with a speculative and searching eye, found an occasion to speak to the bishop concerning the main object of his visit; but the quest was marred by no unseemly haste. The city was eager to proffer hospitality, its guests graciously disposed to accept this. The emperor was lodged in spacious apartments in the palace of the count, the high ranking ecclesiastics who had accompanied him in similar ones in the palace of the bishop; the noblemen were given suitable accommodations with local dignitaries. The soldiery, except for the portion of it that remained on guard duty, set up its tents outside the city's gates. Soon satisfying and savory scents, suggestive of abundance, rose from their soup kettles and their roasting spits and mingled with the crisp night air, while the cold stone walls, which towered behind them, glowed with reflected warmth from their camp fires. It was a time of relaxation as well as anticipation for all concerned, and there was feasting and music and much general good cheer.

But Charlemagne was by no means diverted from his purpose. The following day he began to examine all available documents, and to confer with such members of the clergy and the laity as might have the expert knowledge to help him in his search. Several places were regarded as having been possibilities for hiding the sacred relics, but no one seemed able to give precise information as to the locality of the *Antrum Antiquum* of cherished tradition. At the end of several days, Charlemagne began to fear that perhaps it would be necessary to start the excavations more or less at random. Then he came to a decision, which had been reached less as a result of listening to sage but vague counsel than of offering fervent prayers for Divine guidance: the excavations should begin, he said, directly under the high altar.

Again a great gathering assembled, grouped around the designated place where stalwart laborers were standing, mattocks in hand, awaiting the signal to begin their delving. The bishop offered prayer, Charlemagne raised his hand, and the sound of the mattocks, striking against solid stone, rang out and echoed through the building. But only a small portion of the pavement had been removed, when the quality of the sound changed; it was no longer sharp but dull. As the loosened stones were pried away from the underlying ground and the workmen dug deeper, the sound became strangely hollow. There was a breathless moment of silence. Then came the rush of suppressed air suddenly released, as the crumbling earth parted to disclose a dark cavity which, when illumined, revealed a short flight of steps leading to a passage which wound away into the dim distance. . . .

The emperor and the bishop looked wordlessly at each other. Then together they descended the steps, accompanied only by a chosen few, including torch bearers to light their progress. Cautiously they made their way along and carefully they examined the walls as they went. But these, barren of ornament, gave no clue to the secret, and the zealots continued their search. It was only when the light from the torches, momentarily raised higher than before, flickered over the ceiling of the passageway, that the awed searchers beheld a stone graven with a flowering tree and a fruitful vine, and beside this slab one carved with the words:

Antulfus, Alif, Anselmus, Alboinus, Berardus, sac. vel. cl.

XII

This striking episode, like so many others relating to St. Anne, has more than one version. Personally, as I have said before, I am always inclined to favor the one which seems based on reason and substantiated fact, rather than the one based on sentiment and story. But I still feel bounden to present all available items of our silver treasure, those which are contradictory as well as those which agree and, in the former case, to invite the reader to choose between them—or, if he prefers, to reject them both. Moreover, I am no longer fearful that a dual presentation may cause confusion, for there is now no question of interrupting a normal flow of narrative which treats of events in their natural order. We have so nearly reached the end of our story that an interruption of it becomes of little consequence, compared to that of setting forth, fully and freely, every possible aspect of it.

Here then is that other version of Charlemagne's great discovery, the version given by Monsignor Dubreil, Archbishop of Avignon, in his pastoral letter announcing the crowning of St. Anne in 1876. According to the Reverend Myles Ronan, to whom I myself am indebted for the account, it agrees with the one given in the ancient Breviary of Apt by Monsignor Nicolai, Bishop of that city in 1632:

"It is related that Charlemagne, having concluded one of his many expeditions, had returned to Apt. But it is not known whether his visit was for the purpose of placing his sword beside that of Caesar on the coat of arms of Apt or of being present at the consecration of the cathedral. As this church was one of the forty churches he had promised to build if victory crowned his expeditions, it would seem that Providence wished him to be present as a witness of the miraculous discovery of the relics. On Easter Sunday in the year 792, the Emperor assisted at the Divine Office, surrounded by the faithful and his knights. Suddenly, a youth, blind and a deaf-mute from birth, son of a lord of the

place named Caseneuve de Simiane, came into the church like one inspired and led by an invisible hand. The congregation, evidently also
inspired, immediately rose up instinctively and followed him to the
steps of the sanctuary. By gestures he requested a stone slab to be lifted
and the place to be dug up. The Emperor, who shared in the general
excitement, ordered the boy to be obeyed. Accordingly, the stone was
removed and digging was begun, and soon the crypt was discovered
where lay the relics, and whence bright rays issued.

"Through an opening the cypress coffer was seen, and a bright light
illumined the place. Then a prodigy was witnessed which is worthy of
being recalled side by side with that by which the True Cross was
recognized by S. Helena. The young man, suddenly cured, cried out:
'It is she. . . .' And Charlemagne, greatly excited, also cried out: 'It is
she.' The same words were repeated by the people who fell on their
knees and broke into tears. In fact, in the coffer was found a winding
sheet, that enclosed the relics, on which were inscribed those words
that dispelled all doubt: 'Here lies the body of St. Anne, Mother of the
Glorious Virgin Mary.' "

In presenting this version, Father Ronan remarks that it is "useful
to quote the words" of that great Cardinal, Merry del Val, to the effect
that "tradition, wisely controlled, even in the absence of written documents, gives us manifest proofs of the truths of our beliefs." With this
distinguished and enlightened viewpoint, I am in humble and hearty
accord; and, whether the relics of St. Anne were discovered through
research and perseverance or by a miracle; whether by means of the
carving on stone slabs or of the letters embroidered on a winding
sheet,[31] there seems to be little or no difference of opinion as to what
happened next: Charlemagne ordered that the relics should be reverently gathered together and a careful inventory immediately made of
them. Then a Service of Thanksgiving was held; and the following day
the discovery was officially celebrated at a Mass sung by Archbishop
Turpin, who had accompanied the emperor throughout his journey-
ings and his search. We are told that there was great rejoicing among
the populace of Apt, as well there might have been; also that "according

to his habit," Charlemagne distributed portions of the relics among his friends and reserved for himself that part which he wished to take with him to Aix-la-Chapelle. Then he prepared a *proces verbal* of the inventory and stamped it with his seal; made a report to the Pope in the form of a letter; confided the care of the ossuary to the Bishop of Apt and his successors; and himself continued on his way to his capital, accompanied by his suite and bearing his treasure with him.

From that day to this, Apt has been regarded as the final resting place of Our Lord's grandmother. True, the claim of many other localities to the possession of authentic relics must be regarded as valid, but "the sanctuary of Apt, honored by so many Popes, kings, saints and innumerable pilgrims,[32] is historically and logically the first of the sanctuaries of St. Anne, the benign grandmother of the human race."[33] It is also true that the relics at Apt itself have several times been moved and differently disposed; they are now inclosed in a reliquary formed like a bust which surmounts the altar in the Chapel Royal of the cathedral at Apt. But this very reliquary has a lovely and lasting link with the stone slab engraved with a fruitful vine: every year, on St. Anne's Feast Day, it is decorated with fresh grapes which are afterward taken out and distributed among the sick as "the grapes of St. Anne."

Without mental reservation, but with heartfelt conviction and firm faith, we may say amen to the words of the devout French writer[34] who declared, "If nature and history have done a great deal for Provence, religion has done even more. A place was reserved for it in the distribution of Divine graces on earth, a unique place, as if it bore the last imprint of the life of Jesus Christ among us."

Reliquary of St. Anne, St. Anne's Cathedral, Apt.

*St. Anne and the Virgin. Gilded wood statue in the
Cathedral at Vence, in Provence, not far from Apt.*

PART II.

Cult of St. Anne

The Madonna and Child, St. Anne and Mary, St. Elizabeth and St. John. Church of Santa Maria Antigua, Rome. (This fresco, probably dating from the eighth century, is the oldest known representation of St. Anne.)

I

The Cult of St. Anne—that is to say, her veneration through rites and ceremonies—goes back a long way, and it was general in the Orient before it began in the Occident. This is not surprising when we remember that the first two Bishops of Jersualem, St. James the Less and St. Simon, were her nephews and that the former was probably the author of the Protevangelium; they would naturally have borne witness to the exceptional qualities of any and all persons connected with their Saviour through ties of blood and friendship, and done their utmost to keep the memory of such persons alive. Both these bishops suffered martyrdom, but not until they had reached a very advanced age—indeed, St. James is believed to have been over a hundred years old when he was crucified. Van der Vliet assures us that the "perpetuity of an important Christian community at Jerusalem guarantees the survival up to the year 135 of authentic souvenirs touching the life and survival of Jesus and the principal events of the Infant Church." Then he adds, "Every unprejudiced person will admit without hesitation that the family of Jesus and Christianity at Jerusalem are interwoven with the history of these places."

"The family of Jesus" of course included His grandmother, and the early stories about her were not a matter of mere speculation; they had a firm foundation. Very naturally, they were also the source of admiration, inspiration and, eventually, of veneration. A church was dedicated to her in Constantinople toward the middle of the sixth century; and at the time of the Mussulman Occupation at Jerusalem—636— there was already a Christian church on the site of her home. Similar shrines quickly became numerous throughout the Near East and then the cult spread westward. The discovery of some frescoes, depicting St. Anne, in the Church of Santa Maria Antigua—a basilica in the Forum which had been lost to view since the tenth century and found only as the result of recent excavations—reveals that her cult had already flourished in Rome for some time before the disappearance of the church, as experts have placed the date of the frescoes themselves much earlier than the tenth century. (These are, incidentally, the earliest known representations of St. Anne.) Charlemagne's discovery at Apt of course gave great impetus to her veneration; and, since there were close commercial ties between the two countries even then, it spread rapidly from Provence to Great Britain, where Christianity was already firmly established.

This firm establishment was doubtless due in large measure to the attitude of the great Pope, St. Gregory, whose viewpoint and counsel were as wise as they were humane. When writing to Abbot Mellitus in 601, "he directed that existing temples were to be purified and changed into Christian churches so that 'the nation, seeing their temples are not destroyed, may remove error from their hearts, and knowing and adoring the true God, may the more familiarly resort to the places to which they have been accustomed.' Thus it was that our oldest churches [in England] were built on Celtic holy mounds or close to barrows and stone circles, and that heathen springs, now changed into saints' wells, continued to be visited by devout Christian folk for centuries. The newly baptized people might renounce the old gods with fervor, but they clung to their traditional haunts, and St. Gregory was too wise to forbid them. 'There is no doubt,' he wrote in the same sensible letter of instructions, 'that it is impossible to efface everything at once from their obdurate minds; because he who endeavors to ascend the highest places rises by degrees or steps, and not by leaps.' "[35]

Under such benign spiritual sponsorship, Christianity made rapid strides and, from the very beginning, there was great devotion to St. Anne. Her name was given not only to churches and chapels, but to large numbers of towns, villages, guilds and individuals. Among the most arresting monuments to her cult was a chapel dedicated to "St. Anne, Mother of our Lady," erected in the thirteenth century on a tiny island in the Thames, halfway between Reading Abbey and Caversham —both only little villages. The Benedictines of the Abbey decided to span the river with a bridge and make the "halfway house" at the widest point a place of worship. Upon hearing of this undertaking, King Henry III commanded that an oak should be sent from the Royal

Forest of Windsor to provide wood for the chapel roof, and the little sanctuary soon became the center of great devotion. It was a "free" chapel, that is, not attached to any particular parish, and was served by the Benedictine Monks of the Abbey.

This charming little place was only one of the many dedicated to St. Anne, for, as I have said, her cult spread rapidly; but it was through one of the "heathen springs" which early became "saints' wells" that it achieved its greatest fame. This well, which still exists and still bears her name, is at Buxton in Derbyshire. For centuries, it was a place of pilgrimage for the sick and ailing, and the scene of apparently miraculous cures, as well as great devotion. But alas! the rapacity of King Henry VIII bore no relation to the benevolence of St. Gregory. It finds expression in the order given by his Vicar General, Thomas Cromwell,[36] to the effect that:

"Ecclesiastical persons shall take away, utterly extinct and destroy all shrines, coverings of shrines, tables, candlesticks, trindles or rolls of wax, pictures, paintings, and all other monuments of feigned miracles, pilgrimages, idolatry, and superstition, so that there remain no memory of the same on walls, glasses, windows, or elsewhere within their churches or houses, and they shall exhort all their parishoners to do the like within their several houses."

In the case of St. Ann's Shrine at Buxton these orders were all too faithfully executed, as a letter from Sir William Bassett, a minion of Cromwell's, fully reveals:

"Ryght honorabull my inesspeyciall gud lord, acordyng to my bownden dewte and the teynor of yowre lordschypys lettres lateley to me dyrectyd, I have sende unto youre gud lordschyp by thys beyrer, my brother, Francis Bassett, the ymages of sentt Anne of Buxtone and sentt Mudwen of Burton apon Trentt, the wych ymages I dyd take frome the place where they dyd stande, and brought them to my owne howss within XLVIII houres after the contemplacion of youre seyd lorschypis lettres, in as soober maner as my lyttull and rude wytt wollde serve me. And ffor that there schullde no more idollatre and supersticion be there usyd, I dyd not only deface the tabernaculles and placis where they dyd stande, but also dyd take away cruchys, schertes, and schetes, with wax offeryed, being thynges thatt dyd alure and intyse the yng-norantt pepull to the seyd offerying, allso gyffyng the kepers of both places admonicion and charge thatt no more offeryng schulld be made in those placis tyll the kinges plesure and youre lordschypis be ffurther knowen in that behallf. My lord, I have allso lokkyd up and sealyd the bathys and wells at Buxtons, thatt non schall enter to wasche them, tyll youre lordschypis plesure be ffurther knowne, whereof I besych youre gud lordschyp that I may be ascertanyd off agayn att youre plesure, and I schall not fayle to execute yowre lordschipis cummand-mentt to the uttermust of my lyttull wytt and power. And, my lord, as concernyng the opynion of the pepull and the ffonde truste that they dyd putt in those ymages, and the vanyte of the thynges, thys beyrer my brother cann telle your lordschyp much better att large than I can wryte, for he was with me att the doing of all, and in all placis, as knowyth Jhesu, whome ever have youre Gud lordschyp in his blessyd kepyng. Wrytten at Langley, with the rewde and sympyll hande of youre assuryd and feythfull Orator, and as on ever att your cummand-mentt next unto the kyng to the uttermust of my lyttul power."

WILLIAM BASSETT, knyght.

No doubt this iconoclast felt smugly satisfied that his work of destruc-tion had been complete; instead, though St. Ann's Chapel and her miraculous status had disappeared, the former holy well reappeared as a spa, and was highly recommended to the ailing, along with others in Derbyshire, by a certain Dr. Jones, who, in 1572, wrote a book called *The Benefites of the Auncient Bathes of Buckstones.* "The Earl of Shrewsbury built a bath house there, 'foursquare, four storeys high, so well compact with houses of office, beneath and above and round-about, with a great chamber and other goodly lodgings to the number of thirty' and appointed a resident physician to attend upon the many distinguished people, including Mary, Queen of Scots, who came thither in search of health. . . . However, it was not to St. Ann or any other saint that most of them looked for health, but to the mineral salts in the water and the resident physician's skill. They expected no miracles and left no votive offerings; and if, as was usual, they first asked God's blessing on their enterprise and then returned thanks in the parish church for their cure, that was religion's only connection with the matter."[37]

I wonder?

"The old order changeth, yielding place to new,
And God fulfills Himself in many ways,
Lest one good custom should corrupt the world."

Personally, I cannot help feeling that St. Ann's Well is still an instrument of such fulfillment, even if it is no longer a shrine in the strict sense of the word. To be sure, the everyday visitor who sips a glass of tepid water at the modern, marble-lined springhouse may not be stirred to any great degree, though this establishment is still known as St. Ann's Well; and perhaps the patient who undergoes treatment at the magnificent spa establishment may neglect to offer suitable prayers before and after taking the thermal baths. But I do not believe that anyone familiar with the annual blessing of St. Ann's Well can feel that the older religious beliefs have been entirely supplanted by modern science, or that the mystic qualities of the place have been entirely lost.

The preparation for this annual blessing takes a unique form: St. Ann's Well, as well as several others in its immediate vicinity, long held to have curative powers, is surrounded by a wooden frame filled with damp clay; and on this clay is mounted a covering of flowers and flower petals, so skilfully arranged as to form a picture with a Biblical setting. These arrangements are called "flower mosaics," and the knowledge of how to "dress" a well with a flower mosaic is considered a craft, for it requires great skill, and has been handed down from father to son throughout many generations. The Buxton Well Dressing Festival usually takes place late in June, and is attended by great numbers of people, coming from near and far; and, beside the Well Dressing Ceremony, it includes various lesser celebrations, which take the form of pageantry, folk dancing and so on. But the focal point is St. Ann's Well, beautifully situated, being opposite the curve of the so-called Crescent, constructed in Doric style and comprising several important buildings—the town's most striking architectural feature—and having as a background a beautiful park, rising in flowered terraces.

Flower mosaic. St. Ann's Well, Buxton.

To this ceremony come both the greatest and the humblest of the land. The present Queen of England, shortly before her accession to the throne, graced it with her presence, accompanied by the Duke of Edinburgh; more recently, the Duke and Duchess of Devonshire have been the ranking guests.[38] Many other celebrities of Church and State are always in attendance. In 1955, the Ceremony of the Blessing was conducted by the Mayor's Chaplain, assisted by several other members of the local clergy; it included the singing of hymns, the reading of Scriptures and the offering of prayers, before the actual Blessing was pronounced. One of the prayers read as follows:

"O God, our heavenly Father, accept our thanks for those who first found these healing waters; and grant Thy blessing to all who come to drink thereof; that, being healed of their pains and infirmities, they may show forth Thy praise, not only with their lips, but in their lives, by giving up themselves to Thy service, and walking before Thee in holiness and righteousness all their days; Through Jesus Christ, our Lord, to Whom with Thee and the Holy Ghost be all honour and glory, world without end.

Amen."

I do not believe that anyone who has heard or read this prayer can feel that St. Ann's Well has lost its ancient significance.

Flower mosaic. St. Ann's Well, Buxton.

Votive Offering from the St. Anne. Rear wall, Memorial Chapel, Ste. Anne de Beaupré.

II

Whatever the opinion of others upon this score may be, the religious significance of St. Anne's most famous shrine on the North American continent has, as far as I know, never been challenged. It is at Beaupré, in the Province of Quebec and near the city by the same name. Its renown is well deserved, from many different viewpoints. Historically, it is extremely interesting, and this gives it importance in the eyes of non-Catholics, as well as Catholics, and even in those of non-believers. It owes its foundation to a vow made by a small group of Breton sailors, who landed there in 1658 after having been saved from shipwreck, and who attributed their rescue to the intervention of St. Anne, to whom they promised a votive offering. The same year, a crippled farmer, who had contributed three small stones to the sailors' chapel "through devotion," was suddenly freed from his painful handicap, and this cure was attributed to a miracle. It is no exaggeration to say that, from that time on, practically every great figure in Canadian history, from Iberville down, has visited the shrine; and many, like him, have made votive offerings there. Nor have the prominent personages whose stories have been closely linked with that of St. Anne's been limited to Canadians; such personages have come from every part of the world. Nevertheless, it has been primarily a shrine for everyone and not for the privileged great and it has been kept singularly free from commercialism. "The shrine is strictly religious and may be visited by all, whether Catholic or non-Catholic, entirely free of charge," the official guide book takes pains to point out. "Any building in Ste. Anne's, where admission is charged or religious articles sold for admission, has no connection with the shrine." It is estimated that since its foundation, three hundred years ago, nearly 30,000,000 persons have gone to it. The lame, the halt and the blind have flocked there with prayerful hope in their hearts, and gone away assuaged if not cured, while actual cures have been many; but this assuagement and these cures have not been limited to bodily ailments. "In this lovely meadow—*beau pré*—nestling at the foot of the lofty Laurentian hills and watered by the mighty St. Lawrence, a mysterious power is ever at work from above, performing physical and—far more important—spiritual cures. Beaupré enjoys a heavenly atmosphere of its own hardly paralleled by any other on earth." This is the way it is described by Father Lefebvre, its Director of Pilgrimages, and this is the way I feel about it myself and the way I am sure countless others do.

Since the original shrine was far too small to accommodate the multitudes which, in ever increasing numbers, sought it out, it was eventually converted into a memorial chapel, in which the original attributes were, as far as possible, preserved. It is quaint and charming in all its appointments and its pictures are especially interesting. Over the main altar is a "miraculous painting," attributed to the famous LeBrun, and

presented in 1666 to the shrine by the Marquis de Tracy, Viceroy of New France. It was a votive offering and represents the Marquis and his wife, dressed like pilgrims and kneeling on either side of their coat of arms, in rapt contemplation of the central figures of St. Anne and the Virgin. Over the side altars are paintings by Brother Luke, Recollect, one depicting St. Anne presenting the Virgin at the temple; the other, by the same artist,

representing St. Joachim in the same act of devotion. (These are especially interesting, to me at any rate, as they are the only ones I have seen
showing the presentation when the Virgin was an infant in swaddling
clothes.) At the rear of the chapel are several pictures, donated at
different periods and painted by different artists, but all depicting the
miraculous rescue of sailors and seafarers by St. Anne.

In front of the memorial chapel is a simple fountain, unimpressive
in itself, but significant because there is a spring of some sort at almost
every great pilgrimage center and Ste. Anne de Beaupré is no exception
to this rule. The whole world is familiar with the spring near the grotto
of Lourdes; and the spring at Ste. Anne d'Auray, though less universally
known, is inseparably connected with that great Breton shrine. The
source of the spring at Ste. Anne de Beaupré is on a nearby hill, close
to the path leading to the Holy Staircase and though "it was only toward the middle of the last century that pilgrims began to make devo-
tional use of its water . . .
many of them have been
signally rewarded. Nor
need this cause astonish-
ment. The water of St.
Anne's spring has evi-
dently, of itself, no power
to cure ailments and in-
firmities, but cannot God
make use of it to work
miracles, if he so desires?
Did not our Lord, in the
Gospels, ordinarily make
use of material things to
perform his miracles? . . .
And a significant coinci-
dence about St. Anne's
spring is that, according

Miraculous painting. Attributed to LeBrun. Main altar, Memorial Chapel, Ste. Anne de Beaupré.

to tradition, St. Anne's house stood nearby the "Probatic Pool" mentioned in the gospel."[39]

The present basilica at Ste. Anne de Beaupré, in which 2,000 can be seated and 8,000 find standing room, is a superb gray stone building, with great jewel colored windows, reminiscent of those at Chartres and Bourges. It has an atmosphere of serenity, as well as spaciousness—partly, I think, because it is uncluttered by a superabundance of the mediocre and the tawdry, in the way of decoration, which so often mars otherwise magnificent cathedrals. The miraculous statue of St. Anne, which stands in the north transept, is very beautiful. It has been rightly said that her face, as shown in this image, expresses the kindness of a mother and the dignity of a queen. On her right arm, she holds the infant Mary. Her left hand points to heaven—the source of the power she shares with her daughter; and at her feet are countless crutches which bear tangible evidence of this power. She wears the brilliant diadem with which she was crowned when Pope Leo XIII proclaimed her Patroness of Quebec and she is surrounded by the golden rays which are symbolic of her glory in heaven.

A visit to Ste. Anne de Beaupré is well worth while at any time of year, because of its historic as well as its religious aspects. Personally, I shall always remember with singular emotion the first time I went there, when the roofs as well as the ground were mantled with snow and the sky was as gray as the church. There was such stillness and peace in the place, such a sense of seclusion from the world and such nearness to holy things, that the shrine seemed doubly one of spiritual healing and spiritual revelation. But this may have been partly because I was confused and troubled, and because I was signally in need of the tranquility which, elsewhere, I had sought in vain and which I found there in such abundant measure; I left the church not only composed and comforted, but uplifted. Indeed, this experience marked one of the great turning points in my life; and now, a quarter of a century after it took place, I still recognize its supreme importance to me and give thanks.

I believe that anyone whose need is solitude and silence, as mine was then, would find solace and succor at Ste. Anne de Beaupré on such a winter's day. But to those whose souls' sincere desire is rather to participate in a great ceremonial, and thus achieve the sensation of shared privileges and shared benefits, I think that unquestionably the most moving experience at St. Anne's, especially for women with young daughters and granddaughters, is to be found at a celebration on September 8th, traditionally the Virgin's birthday.

For this feast of the maternity of St. Anne, as Father Lefebvre, Director of Pilgrimages at Beaupré,[40] has reminded us, is also, vicariously, the feast day of all Christian mothers; and the most impressive part of the program consists of the candlelight procession in which many such mothers and their young daughters—or grandmothers with their young granddaughters—participate. A large section of the great basilica has been reserved for them, and they assemble there to sing and pray and listen to a sermon especially directed toward their responsibilities and their privileges before they begin their joyous and triumphant march. They sit with their shaded candles still unlit, until the signal to illumine these is given; then, suddenly, throughout the church, the lights begin bursting into bloom, like great glowing tulips, until the nave is radiant with them. Gradually, the procession begins to form, with clergy and choristers falling into line and banners and relics reverently borne along. A few of the daughters who have entitled their mothers to a place in this proud company are still so small that they are carried close to the maternal breast; many are wearing the veiled white of their First Holy Communion; none have passed their first eager and hopeful youth. Among the marching mothers and grandmothers, some are hardly out of their teens, some are already pushing middle age, and some are well along in years. For the most part, they apparently belong to what we call, for the sad lack of a better term, the plain people. There is no elegance of dress among them, nor is their feminine charm enhanced by various picturesque costumes, as it is at Ste. Anne d'Auray; they wear serviceable, warm woollens, for in September it is already cool in Canada, and, for the most part, these woolens seem rather drab in color and uninspired in cut to the outsider who is an onlooker among them. The only display of jewels in the basilica is in the crowns destined to be placed on the miraculous statue, after the procession is over. But these women who are sharing the feast of St. Anne's maternity, like the mother of the Gracchi, have other jewels; and the faces under the simple scarves and nondescript hats are alight with happiness and faith. This is indeed their day, too, as well as the day of the "Good Ste. Anne," which is what they always call her, as naturally as they speak of *Le Bon Dieu*. They rejoice and are glad in it.

Miraculous Statue. Ste. Anne de Beaupré.

Statue of Ste. Anne d'Auray.

III

Strangely enough—or is it really strange? Is it perhaps one of those parts of a sublime pattern which seem to fit so perfectly into place?— the devotion at the shrine of Ste. Anne d'Auray, the most famous in Europe, began at almost the same time that it began at Ste. Anne de Beaupré. It was in 1623, only thirty-five years before the small group of stranded Breton sailors landed safely on the beautiful meadow in Quebec, after averting shipwreck through the intervention of St. Anne, that Yves Nicolazic, a Breton peasant who lived near Auray in Brittany itself, announced that St. Anne had appeared to him in a vision; that she had instructed him to build a chapel in her honor on a nearby field; and that she had told him a similar chapel had existed there nearly a thousand years earlier. At first his story, which he kept reiterating, was treated with scorn, and he himself was the object of widespread ridicule; but a sudden change in this attitude took place, when a primitive statue of the saint, in a damaged condition, was unearthed in the very field that Nicolazic had designated! Offerings immediately poured in and a chapel was promptly built, where the rescued image was placed and entrusted to the care of the Carmelites; but they could not safeguard it against the fury that prevailed during the French Revolution. It suffered further damage, and the more important and spacious buildings and the beautiful cloister which, by then, supplemented the original chapel were also partially destroyed. In the middle of the nineteenth century, however, reconstruction began on a grandiose scale and in a grandiose manner. A great basilica now stands on the site of Nicolazic's discovery; the humble peasant has been given a glorious tomb there; and the broken remains of the statue so miraculously found have been enshrined beside an altar of modern workmanship.

Instead of being hemmed in by lesser buildings, like so many European cathedrals, this one is surrounded by a vast expanse of open space. Opposite it, but at a considerable distance, is a so-called Scala Santa, or Holy Staircase, where open air services are sometimes held, and which pilgrims ascend on their knees in the same way that they do the original one in Rome; while, at right angles to the basilica, at the rear of the enclosure as large as a ball park and surrounded by a low stone wall, is the *Monument aux Morts*—the monument of the dead. Here each of the five Breton dioceses is represented by an altar in the crypt; and this in turn is surmounted by an arcaded rotunda, reached from the outside by twin curving staircases, where Mass is celebrated on certain important occasions.

The most important of all these, very naturally, is the feast of St. Anne, which falls on July 26th. All day long, on the 25th, pilgrims have been arriving from far and wide; and in the evening there has been a recitation of the rosary in the basilica, and a torchlight procession starting from there, wending its way to the Scala Santa, on to the *Monument aux Morts,* and back to the basilica again. Throughout this ceremony I was constantly reminded of the similar one I had seen at Ste. Anne de Beaupré: again a great gray church, again a vast assemblage of plainly dressed, devout people, again the shaded candles suddenly bursting into bloom like orange-colored flowers. But the next day, instead of being reminiscent of another shrine, this one assumed its own unique character.

The first Mass in the basilica was at three in the morning; many had remained to spend the night in prayer after marching in the torchlight procession and were, therefore, already on hand to attend this Mass and those which followed it in rapid succession. Then, very early in the morning, crowds began pouring in from every direction, with the immense enclosure facing the *Monument aux Morts* as their objective. *"Les Bretons sont tres croyants,"* I have heard it frequently said. This may be translated in two ways: either "The Bretons are very credulous," and that is what those who are without faith themselves mean when they say it; or "The Bretons are very devout"—and that is what others mean. It is what I myself have every reason to mean when I say it, for I have witnessed this great devotion in full measure on St. Anne's fete.

It was a day of sunshine but strong wind and warm clothing was a requisite; but now its drabness was relieved by the characteristic *coiffes* —those elaborate Breton headdresses of ancient origin, a different one for every locality, which still crowned many of the older women and some of the younger ones, although alas! their general use is disappearing. Nevertheless, so great is their quaintness and charm that the fortunate observer is constantly on the alert to discover more and more of them, in ever differing forms. All are alike in their delicate textures of sheer muslin, embroidery and lace and in their snowy whiteness; but there all likeness ends. Some are as simple and as close fitting as a baby's bonnet; some lie flat on the head like a pancake; some are wide winged, waving in unison with the brisk breeze; some rise tall and cone shaped above a well-set head and are firmly tied beneath a shapely chin; some have blue ribbons or pink ribbons or white ribbons fluttering out behind them like gay banners. It is just as well that, at the time of our arrival at Ste. Anne d'Auray on July 26th, the hour at which religious services are to begin is still far off; otherwise, we might not give these our undivided attention. Our gaze is fixed and our interest centered on the demure *coiffe* of Nantes, on the flighty *coiffe* of Fouesnant, the charming one of Vannes, the fantastic one of Bigoudenne and a score of others.

But the *coiffes* are not all that we are bent on observing as we set up our camp chairs just outside the low stone wall, at an admirable vantage point. Traditionally, the basic dress to wear with these *coiffes,* all over Brittany, is a simple one of black velvet, combined with black satin, and made with a tight fitting bodice, a full skirt and long, full sleeves; to this various collars, aprons, shawls and ornaments are added at will. There are not as many of these in evidence or in as great diversity as when I first went to Brittany, many years ago; but every now and then a bodice or an apron or a shawl, bright as to color, ornate as to embroidery, comes into view. Rarer than the feminine figures which set these off are those of the men who still wear the flat beaver hats, with rolling brims and small streamers, along with velveteen jackets and breeches cut after a regional fashion; but there are still a few of these, too. This is the day of days in Brittany; whatever does most honor to its patroness on her fete, that will be done by her faithful followers, according to their lights; and if they feel they can best do this by following the customs of their ancestors, in dress as well as in devotion, this is the method they will choose.

Late in the morning, an announcement is made from the pulpit, over the loud speaker, that the great enclosure must not be used for picnicking. But that is not until long after many a hungry pilgrim has followed another time honored custom: that of setting up a small folding table, which seems to come from nowhere, surrounding it with folding chairs or stools, which likewise have come out of the blue, and settling down to a hearty meal whose previous accommodation is also a mystery. There are hundreds of these well-equipped picnickers to be seen along every country road in France on a sunny day and on some that are not so sunny. They are eating between the hours of twelve and two, sacred to lunch; they are eating again between the hours of four and five, set aside for that strange sweet snack known as *gouter;* and they begin to eat after seven and continue until the long twilight has been engulfed in darkness, which is not until well after nine in summer —for all of that period is dinner time. On St. Anne's feast day the little folding tables begin to make their appearance as early as nine in the morning—for the Pontifical Mass is to begin at ten-thirty and many of these pilgrims have come a long way to attend it and have breakfasted early and lightly before they set out. I, for one, am glad to see them enjoying themselves in their normal way; and I think St. Anne would have felt the same about it!

The crowds grow greater and greater, the little tables are folded up and put away, since there is no room for them any more. But the little camp stools remain upright, for no seats are provided by those in charge of the ceremonies, and only the pilgrims who have brought their own with them can sit down. Occasionally, one such pilgrim, sheltered from the wind by the wall, continues to munch contentedly a huge sandwich, made of crusty bread sliced lengthwise, with well-larded ham or hunks of strong cheese for a filling; but for the most part people are on the move now and are coming in groups: boy scouts led by a priest, who sing as they take their places on the grass; school girls in charge of a nun, whose habit is as unfamiliar and as picturesque as that which the coiffed laywomen are wearing; a procession headed by a banner inscribed, "The Crusade of the Blind," in which the marchers come two by two—those who cannot see led, in each case, by those who can, with infinite tenderness and care. There are babies in arms with their mothers and fathers, and old men and women, many of them bent with age, accompanied by sturdy, upright sons and daughters, themselves already aging. There were scores in the great enclosure when we came, then hundreds; now there are thousands.

There is a sudden surge toward the portal of the basilica, and crowds press closer and closer to the cleared avenue leading toward the *Monument aux Morts*. The procession, headed by its crucifer, its choir and its acolytes, is leaving the church. It includes four abbots, nine bishops, an archbishop and a cardinal, besides a papal vicar and several distinguished laymen with honorary papal titles. The most precious and beautiful banners have been taken from the sacristy for this occasion, and the golden statue of St. Anne, inclosed in a gold-framed and gold-lidded *vitrine,* is borne triumphantly aloft. Only the spearheads atop the staffs of the banners, only the golden lid of the *vitrine,* only the heads and shoulders of the dignitaries are visible as the cortege moves majestically along its appointed way in the midst of the multitudes; it affords a mere glimpse of crimson and scarlet, a flash of gilding, a flutter of embroidery and lace; but, as the ascent of the curving staircase begins, the pageantry is revealed in all its magnificence. The bishops are vivid figures now; the cardinal's great mantle streams out behind him in a flow of color. The great moment for those who have waited so long has arrived, the goal of those who have journeyed so far has been reached. The Pontifical Mass is about to begin.

Of course, this does not mark the end of the fete. When the Mass is over and the venerated statue, the embroidered banners, the dignitaries who have come from near and far—one of the bishops is a Chinese—have disappeared within the basilica again, the crowds will disperse, to wander about among the stalls where foodstuffs and souvenirs of all sorts are sold, to greet their friends, and to have an interval of merrymaking before vespers and the reluctant and weary return to the places whence they have come. But in a sense, pleasant as all this may be, it is an anticlimax. The culmination and core of the festival was in the morning's Mass. And that, I believe, is as it should be.

The pre-eminent position enjoyed by this feast, as celebrated at Ste. Anne d'Auray, may easily be gauged by the fact that the Pope, who, all his life, has excelled as a linguist, recently added Breton to the many tongues he can command, in order to address the faithful of Brittany in their own language. Elsewhere listeners over the radio were both baffled and startled when, at the end of a July 26th broadcast, prepared and delivered especially for his Breton audience, he pronounced the following words:

"Revo melet kalon glan Mari.
"Revo melet Santez Anna patronez vad er vretoned."

But the pilgrims assembled at Ste. Anne d'Auray and their compatriots throughout the province, who were prevented from being present but who were eagerly listening in, knew that he was saying:

"Praise be to the Immaculate Heart of Mary.
"Praise be to St. Anne, patroness of the Bretons."

And fresh joy surged through them at the knowledge that the Holy Father was with them in spirit and in truth and that he had given new glory to their own form of speech.

In possession of the author
St. Anne and the Virgin. Quimper pottery.

IV

Admittedly, the celebration of St. Anne's feast day at the shrine dedicated to her in New Orleans is much simpler, much more localized in sentiment and arrangement, than either the celebration at Ste. Anne de Beaupré or the one at Ste. Anne d'Auray. There, in late July, are no brisk winds with which to contend; but on the other hand there is the intense and humid heat of the Deep South in midsummer and sudden and violent showers. There is the inevitable lack of space for great crowds in the very heart of a teeming metropolis, the absence not only of a beautiful landscape and picturesque costumes, but of that special atmosphere which comes from long tradition. Nevertheless, it is also extremely impressive. The procession which leaves the church on the night of July 26th attempts to do no more than encircle the city block that comprises the property of the Archconfraternity—which includes a Scala Santa—and return to the church. But a non-Catholic who had come, at my suggestion, to see this spectacle, merely as a bystander, was so moved by it that he wrote me afterward in this vein:

"The chanting of the praying congregation streamed from the church windows and blended with the normal sounds of a mellow evening. The warm light from the church door gilded the sidewalks and trees around it. The faces of the passers-by were lighted in the same glow; some stopped and looked in, and you could see their expressions change and soften, as if, for a fleeting moment, they, too, felt they belonged to the flock within. Some hurried along, crossing themselves as they passed the church door; but some scurried by, heads down, faces averted, as if guilt and shame drove them on.

"The singing in the church rose to a climax and gently fell. The congregation began to move slowly toward the door, and as each worshipper emerged, he reached for a lighted candle from the racks which stood near the entrance. When the procession formed, those who took part in it seemed to lose their identity and to merge into the semi-darkness of the night, only the flickering lines of lighted candles showed the vague figures of the marchers as they moved down the street and turned again to re-enter the church. But as they returned, their faces seemed lighted by more than the radiance from the open door. Those of the young glowed with emotion, as if they were eager to share their joy with others who might benefit by their great act of devotion. The more mature faces were solemn, humble and forceful, as if mindful of borne burdens, yet able to carry these. The faces of the old showed relief at the nearness to a journey's end and the realization that they were coming home."

Attendance at a ceremony as moving and impressive as this naturally leads to awakened interest regarding regional devotion to St. Anne—or St. Ann, as many Orleanians prefer to spell her name—and I quickly consulted Roger Baudier, the eminent authority I have previously mentioned, for further enlightenment. I was not surprised when he wrote me, in a friendly letter, "We owe much of the spread of the devotion to St. Ann here in Louisiana to the French priests from Brittany who served in this state in previous decades. Brittany probably gave more priests to the church in the state than any other part of France." This I already partly knew and partly divined, and my own findings in connection with the story of St. Anne had been the same as his, namely that "the legend is encountered over and over again in the works of the early writers, especially in the East. Practically all the information we have about St. Anne in the early centuries comes from the Apochryphal Gospels, generally known as the Oriental Legend." But I was unprepared for many of the historical details which he was good enough to attach to his letter in the form of a memorandum:

"Devotion to St. Ann was introduced into Louisiana during the French colonial period by settlers from France. This is evident from the frequent appearance of that saint's name in Baptismal registers—Marie-Anne, Anne, Anna, Anne-Marie, Marianne, etc. When the French engineer for the Company of the Indies, Sieur de Pauger, laid out the plans for New Orleans in 1722, he designated one of the streets as 'la Rue Sainte Anne,' and it has remained St. Ann Street to this day.

"During the episcopal administrations of Monseigneur de Neckere,

Monseigneur Antoine Blanc, Monseigneur Jean-Marie Odin and Monseigneur Napoleon Joseph Perche, many French priests from Brittany volunteered for service in the Louisiana mission field, also many from the Lyons area. Both sections of France are particularly noted for their intense devotion to St. Ann. These priests promoted devotion to St. Ann, not only in New Orleans, but also in the rural areas. St. Ann societies began to be formed in some parishes for married women. Holy Trinity Church at New Orleans has an old St. Ann Society. A number of priests also came down from Canada to labor in French-speaking Louisiana, and they too fostered devotion to St. Ann, so widely practiced in their native northland.[41]

"When Archbishop Antoine Blanc decided to establish a new parish in the rear of New Orleans in 1852, to care for the growing number of Catholics who were establishing themselves around and beyond Claiborne Avenue and along 'la Route du Bayou' (Bayou Road), the new church was placed under the invocation of St. Ann. . . . It still stands, now serving as St. Peter Claver Church for a Negro congregation under the Josephite Fathers. St. Ann's Parish Church was moved and established at the present location on Ursulines Avenue in 1920. It was always the center of devotion to that saint and the feast was regularly observed every July 26th with due solemnities. However, it was left to the fourth pastor of St. Ann's, Very Rev. John B. Bogaerts, and a French priest from Brittany, Father Hattais, to give impetus to the devotion through the establishment of a shrine. The incidents and circumstances that led to this are best told in Father Bogaerts' own words, preserved in the parish annals.

" 'Father Hattais, a Breton by birth, had imbibed the devotion to St. Ann from his childhood and he never preached a sermon during the Lenten season without kindly referring to the Saint of his choice and without invoking her blessing on his apostolic labors. He never tired of speaking of the power and goodness of St. Ann, of the many spiritual and temporal favors which he and others had received through the intercession of good St. Ann, and how the devotion of St. Anne d'Auray had been the means of preserving and strengthening the Faith in his own native Brittany.

" 'It was thought that if St. Ann were honored in a special manner in this part of the world, she would in a similar way display here her power and her goodness. Had she not done so already in other places of the New World, at Ste. Anne de Beaupré, Quebec, and at St. John's Church, 76th Street, New York, where far-famed shrines of St. Ann exist? Through this devotion, numberless souls have been led back to God and the Christian spirit had been revived in families where it was well nigh extinct.

" 'It was further argued that the erection of a shrine of St. Ann would be the fittest way to commemorate the Golden Jubilee of the Parish, which occurs this year (1902), and an appropriate means of infusing new life into the Parish; also that the Shrine might become a center of religious activity from which the devotion to good St. Ann might radiate over the Southern country, and wherever favors obtained at this shrine might become known.'

"The plan for the shrine was announced to the women of the parish at a time when they were making a retreat. The project was received with enthusiasm, and a meeting for them and for the men of the parish was scheduled for the following Sunday. Within a few months a substantial sum of money had been collected and many special gifts had been made. To promote further devotion, Father Bogaerts organized a Confraternity of St. Ann, which was formally approved by Archbishop Chapelle. He also approved the rules of the Confraternity and the prayer of consecration to that saint; and on November 9, 1902, the beautiful shrine of St. Ann in the parish church was formally blessed. That same evening marked the first meeting of the Confraternity of St. Ann.

"Not long after the establishment of the parish, a relic, supported by authenticating documents, was given to the church by Bishop Portiere of Mobile. This relic is regularly venerated by devotees of St. Ann at this shrine, and is carried in the outdoor procession every year on the feast of St. Ann.

"In 1916 Father Bogaerts resigned and the Rev. Francis Badeaux became pastor. While on a visit to Rome in 1925, he petitioned the Holy See through the Sacred Congregation of the Council to elevate the Confraternity of St. Ann to the rank of Archconfraternity. This was done by Pope Pius XI through a Brief dated May 18, 1926, authorizing the society to aggregate to itself other St. Ann societies throughout the United States. *The Archconfraternity, accordingly, is the highest St. Ann confraternity in the United States."*

Certainly this is a record of achievement which every Catholic can read with admiration, and in which every southern Catholic has reason to feel special pride—coupled with a great sense of debt to Brittany! And as a reminder of the signal honor bestowed on this parish, *St. Ann's Herald,* its official organ, reprints every month the translation of the Papal Brief which elevated the Confraternity of St. Ann of New Orleans to the dignity and rank of an Archconfraternity by order of Pope Pius XI. I feel privileged to quote it in full:

"Within the limits of the Archdiocese of New Orleans, and in the Archepiscopal city, there exists a Sodality of St. Ann, which was erected in the parish church of that name under the same title of St. Ann in the year 1902. This Confraternity flourishes with a large membership, and many of the faithful of Christ visit the sanctuary dedicated to the Mother of the Mother of God in the same parish.

"Now, as the pastor of the above-mentioned church has, with the approval of the Archbishop of New Orleans, earnestly requested that with Apostolic kindness we should elevate this same Sodality to the rank of an Archconfraternity, we have decided to grant this petition. Wherefore, having consulted with their Eminences the Cardinals of the Holy Roman Church appointed to interpret the decrees of the Council of Trent, through the continuance of the present brief, by our Apostolic authority, and in perpetuity, we elevate and promote the Sodality canonically erected under the title of St. Ann in the City of New Orleans and in the parish church there dedicated to the same saint, to the dignity and rank of an Archconfraternity, with the usual privileges.

"And we likewise grant, by virtue of our Apostolic authority, through this present brief, to the directors and members, present and future, of the Sodality herein elevated by us to the rank of an Archconfraternity, that they may in the future aggregate lawfully and freely other societies of the same name erected or to be erected within the limits, however, only of the United States of North America, and that they may communicate to them all the indulgences granted by the Apostolic See to the above-mentioned Archconfraternity.

"These things we hereby grant and command, ordering these present decrees to exist and remain always firm, valid and effective, to have and obtain their full and integral effects, to aid and assist most fully the said Archconfraternity and those others whom it may concern now and forever; and thus must be judged and considered as null and void anything decreed otherwise by anyone, by any authority whatsoever, knowingly or ignorantly, anything to the contrary whatsoever.

"Given at Rome, at St. Peter's, under the Ring of the Fisherman, the 18th day of the month of May, in the year 1926, and in the fifth year of our Pontificate."

J. CARD. GASPARRI, Secretary of State.

Photograph by Elemore Morgan.

Procession leaving St. Anne's Church, New Orleans, on her feast day.

V

I have tried to indicate how deeply moved and greatly impressed I have been by the celebrations of St. Anne's feast day at which I have had the privilege of being present; but I cannot leave the subject without adding that I have also been deeply moved and greatly impressed by the accounts which have reached me of celebrations, both great and small, which were taking place on the same day all over the world.

"On the site where Mass is said to have been first offered in New England in 1666, Bishop Edward F. Ryan of Burlington will preside at a Solemn Mass on July 26, the Feast of St. Anne, mother of the Blessed Virgin. . . . In the afternoon there will be veneration of a relic of St. Anne, Stations of the Cross and Benediction. In preparation for the Feast, parishioners have been making a solemn novena to St. Anne."

So runs a news dispatch from tiny Isle La Motte in Lake Champlain. I know this lovely peaceful site well, so I can easily visualize the scene, even though I have not been there on St. Anne's special day, for all days on Isle La Motte seem to be under her quiet protection. A dispatch from Scranton, Pennsylvania evokes a different, but even more stimulating feeling:

"Marking the close of a novena in honor of Mary's mother, an estimated 150,000 persons visited the grounds of St. Ann's Passionist Monastery here on the Feast of St. Ann.

"Many were on hand early in the morning to hear one of the 50 Masses offered between four and eight o'clock. Many other pilgrims attended novena services throughout the day offered in various languages.

"The transit strike which has tied up all public transportation in Scranton for more than 120 days had little effect on the novena. Attendance was greater than ever before. This may have been due to a 'share-the-ride' plan devised by the Passionist Fathers. Two thousand stickers which read 'Going to St. Ann's Novena' were distributed to persons owning cars prior to the opening of the novena.

"Bishop Jerome D. Hannan of Scranton told a crowd of 75,000 that stayed for the evening service at an outdoor altar that a spirit of friendship for the saints had brought the multitudes to the great novena in honor of St. Ann.

"As in years past, a group of pilgrims made the 10-mile journey from Pittston, Pa., to St. Ann's Monastery on foot. Many joined the line of march from communities the pilgrims passed on their way. Reciting the rosary as they went, they arrived in time for the 5:30 a.m. Mass."

Both of the above reports came to me through the thoughtful kindness of Katharine McKiever, an editor of the N.C.W.C. News Service, who realized that they would have a special significance for me when I myself was at Ste. Anne d'Auray, by giving me a feeling of union with the celebrations that were simultaneously taking place in my own country; and it is through the equally thoughtful kindness of the Director of Pilgrimages at the Breton shrine that I am able to quote from two letters recently received there from French priests in the mission field:

"It is from the deep heart of Africa, more than 5,000 kilometres from France, that this letter comes to you from an Auxiliary Chapel of Ste. Anne d'Auray, who is the patroness of our Mission and whom we venerate with great devotion," writes R. P. Mairot, O.M.I. "True, the 26th of July is not marked here by all the pomp and splendor of your pilgrimage. But we also have our own procession and venerate the little relic which we possess.

"What is more, here in Basutoland, we are very proud to have as part of our Catholic Action an organized branch of the Congregation of *Dames de Ste. Anne* which is of immense help to us in our Apostolate.

"Our mission of Ste. Anne d'Auray in Basutoland is among the Mountains of Drakensberg and is located at an altitude of nearly 2,500 feet. It was founded in 1940 by a Breton priest, Father Victor Guen, was necessarily dormant through the war, but has now begun to advance rapidly. At present, there are two priests here, aided by four nuns, two of whom are native Africans, ministering to a population of about 20,000 inhabitants, of whom 5,000 are Catholics. We, therefore, have an enormous task before us in order to convert all our little world and to make them as fervent Christians as the Bretons.

"That is why I ask today for help and prayers from your pilgrims at Auray for their little sister: the Mission of Ste. Anne d'Auray at Basutoland. I wish that the message from your pilgrimage could come to us in a great outpouring of prayer for the conversion of our heathens and our Protestants, for our Order of the Sacred Heart, for the *Dames de Ste. Anne,* for the Children of Mary, above all for our schools. At the moment, we have ten schools which bring 700 children together; that gives us much anxiety and many problems to solve.

"I do not know whether some time in the future we will have a beautiful basilica, as you do. For the moment, our church, which is combined with our school, is a great hangar covered with zinc, and cluttered with all sorts of materials for future use. But St. Anne does not need to be richly served. Her treasure was in having, as a daughter, the Mother of Jesus. In our poverty, we also hope to form spirits dedicated to Jesus and to Mary.

"It is with the great hope of finding among your pilgrims and your parishioners the spiritual aid which will help us transform our *Basothos* into fervent Christians and develop the service of St. Anne that I send you this letter."

The other letter made available to me at Ste. Anne d'Auray came from the Rev. R. P. Delbos, located at Fujieda in Japan, and reads, in part, as follows:

"How does it happen that this mission, founded in 1878, was put under the patronage of St. Anne? Nobody who is here now knows. Perhaps because of the personal devotion of the missionary founder; perhaps because of the nearness to a church dedicated to the Blessed Virgin. However that may be, this patronage was never merely a matter of title. The oldest Christians around here declare that they have always seen the Feast of St. Anne solemnly celebrated. From the very beginning, it has been a holy day, like Christmas and Easter. On the Vigil of the Feast, a supper has always been prepared in the Presbytery for the Christians of the community, and the evening of the feast there has always been a banquet for the parochial council.

"When the first church, built by Father Tanooka, was blessed, the Bishop of Tokio celebrated a Pontifical Mass here, certainly the only one in this locality.

"What is the present condition of the Mission? Fujieda, a town of 14,000 inhabitants, is the center of a small province of 300,000 inhabitants of whom only 290 are Catholics. There has been a resident priest only since 1939. Evangelization is still to be undertaken. What could we do during the war? Nevertheless, St. Anne has certainly watched over her parish. The church is well preserved, the Christian spirit even better. Despite the relative abandonment of this Christian center, also despite the awakening of the nationalistic spirit in Japan, missionaries and catechists vied with each other in sustaining the faith of Christians and teaching submission to the Holy Father and a spirit of charity. The protection of our patroness extends even to the furthermost buildings. In 1923 a fire broke out in one corner of our house; while firemen were trying to find a way of putting it out, it extinguished itself as if by a miracle.

"At Christmastime, in 1947, Monsignor Wakida, the Bishop of Yokohama, designated me for this post. I had the impression that St. Anne was taking me by the hand and leading me into her domain."[42]

Each in its own way, these accounts have stirred me; and then I came upon two more, both—though in a very different manner—taking advantage of St. Anne's feast day to stress her role as a grandmother; and, of course, these have a special appeal, since that is the role in which I, myself, am primarily considering her.

One of these comes to me from Luray, Virginia, and is contained in *Catholic View*, the weekly bulletin issued in the parish of Our Lady of the Valley. Its wording is informal—almost colloquial—and, therefore, probably all the more likely to find response in the audience it is especially designed to reach:

"HAVE YOU A GRANDMA? HERE'S AN IDEA FOR TUESDAY."

"Do you still have a grandmother here on earth? If you do, you're lucky. Most of us who are a little older have long since lost our grandmothers—and now we feel that loss keenly. But if your grandma is still around, why don't you figure out some especially nice surprise and then spring it on her this coming Tuesday? It will amaze her—naturally— when she sees you going out of your way to please her. And when she wants to know the reason why, you can explain that Tuesday is 'Grandmother's Day.' It's the feast of St. Anne, the grandmother of our Blessed Lord."

The other account comes to me in the form of a sermon, delivered at Lac St. Joseph, Quebec, by the Rev. Bernard Morisset, Professor of Theology at Laval University, who enjoined his congregation to consider St. Anne in her role of a grandmother. "It is this aspect of her personality that I wish to stress today," he said. "Grandmothers are educators of a very special kind. The experience of years, the courage which has been fortified through trial, the appeasement of violent passions, the necessity of adapting one's self to changing eras, the certainty that sunshine will always come after storm: all these qualities give them a particular talent for dealing with children. Grandmothers have an art of their own; they are patient, gentle and long suffering when they take care of children and if they are sometimes inclined to soften parental discipline, they, nevertheless, get surprising results in controlling their small charges. Their method of education is efficacious; and what zeal they show when their grandchildren are sick and what prayers they offer when these cherished children do not always follow in the strait and narrow path! Really, grandmothers are so necessary to children they ought never to die!

"My brothers, is St. Anne not really the embodiment of the grandmother for all mankind, since Mary is the mother of all mankind? Think of the benefits attributed to her: she appeases Divine wrath, she heals the sick, she obtains the grace of conversion; and she is not only the grandmother who cares for our spiritual welfare, but who safeguards the well-being of the family household. The greatest grace which we can ask of St. Anne is to preserve for these households the strength and the virtues which have characterized them in the past."

South portal of the Monastery, Daphni.

VI

A poem about prayer which I have always loved ends with the lines,

"For so the whole wide world is every way
Bound by gold chains about the throne of God."

Not only in visiting shrines dedicated to St. Anne myself, but in reading such accounts as those I have quoted—accounts which have, literally, reached me from throughout the whole wide world—I have come
to feel that women everywhere, and particularly grandmothers everywhere, can meet in spirit at the feet of St. Anne. This feeling is, of
course, particularly strong in connection with the places where her
cult is observed with the same faith and fervor which have long characterized it. But even in places where the observance of this cult has
long since ceased, if it once really existed, the atmosphere still seems
permeated with something mystic and lovely, almost in the same way
that the perfume of flowers may still remain after the flowers themselves have faded and been removed. Outstanding among such places,
at least in my experience, is the beautiful Byzantine Monastery at
Daphni, near Athens.

It is located on the Sacred Road leading to Eleusis, and in all prob-
ability marks the site of an ancient temple dedicated to Apollo, which
was destroyed by the Visigoths when they invaded Greece in 395 A.D.
Several very charming legends surround the monastery's early history.
According to one of them, a queen named Daphne, was shipwrecked
at Aigialos, a short distance from the inland course of the Sacred Road.
As a thank offering to Our Lord's mother for having saved her from
drowning, Queen Daphne built the monastery, giving it her name, and
financing its erection with the treasure contained in twelve barrels full
of valuable cargo which she was carrying in her bark!

This story, though delightful, seems fantastic rather than likely;
nevertheless, the monastery may well be the oldest Christian building

in Attica. Even more probably it was built during the reign of the Emperor Justinian—that is to say, about the middle of the sixth century. Parts of the earlier structure, notably the wall which forms its enclosure, are still intact, though other parts have disappeared. But the greater portion of the church, as it now stands, was doubtless built in the eleventh century, on the occasion of a visit to Athens by Emperor Basilius, and either in his honor or at his command. Certainly the magnificent mosaics, which were the chief glory of the monastery, and which interpret a story which begins with the comforting visit of the angel to Joachim and Anne, and continues through the Crucifixion of Our Lord and the Assumption of the Blessed Virgin, date from this era.

After the conquest of Greece by the Franks, the Orthodox monks were expelled, and the structure was taken over by French Cisterians, who treated its ecclesiastical treasures not only with respect but with reverence, and increased its importance by the addition of several supplementary buildings. Furthermore, the generally high regard in which it was held is apparent from the fact that it became the chosen burial place for the Dukes of Athens, who belonged to the noble family of de la Roche, evidences of whose tombs still remain. Later, the Turkish Occupation of Greece brought the Orthodox monks back again; but during the Insurrection of 1821, the monastery, which was also a fortification, was badly damaged. After that came a sad period of desertion and disintegration; but some seventy years ago, a process of careful and enlightened restoration was begun; and though the church of the erstwhile monastery is now a national monument and not a place of worship, nothing about it suggests neglect, much less decay. The destroyers —the Visigoths and the Turks—seem to have left no mark there. It is the pious monks, both Greek and French, who have stamped it with their seal and permeated it with their spirit; and the subsequent restorers have understood what they have been and done and have sought to interpret and revivify this. The church, sturdy and symmetrical, rises in gray majesty against the sapphire splendor of the Greek sky; laurel trees with glossy leaves grow all around it, as they did when the time-honored place was first given its name—for this is not dependent on the legend of the shipwrecked queen, since the word Daphne, though often used for a proper name means laurel!—and the superb mosaics

The Birth of the Virgin. Mosaic at the Monastery, Daphni.

glow with the same vivid colors which illumined these stone walls a thousand years ago. St. Anne is represented throughout wearing a blue robe and a rose-colored mantle, while St. Joachim is uniformly clad in white; the robes of the attendant angels sometimes match hers and sometimes his. In the panel depicting the presentation at the temple, the high priest is also robed in rose, the little Virgin Mary and her young attendants in very dark blue—a curious and interesting departure from the tradition which tells us they were all white clad. Every one of these mosaics is a masterpiece, both in feeling and in execution; the one depicting the Nativity has a naive quaintness which is very appealing, and it would be hard to tell which of the others is the most compelling. But for the student of St. Anne's life and cult, it is, of course, the panels devoted to her which are of supreme importance; why they have not been more generally visited and more widely

The Promise of a Child to St. Anne and St. Joachim. Mosaic at the Monastery, Daphni.

The Presentation at the Temple. Mosaic at the Monastery, Daphni.

heralded is a mystery to me. I shall always regard the midsummer morning spent at the great national monument which was once her shrine, as well as that of her daughter and her Grandson, to have marked one of the greatest experiences in a long period of travel and research; and this feeling was naturally intensified by the thoughtful gift of the beautiful Tropania used on the several days consecrated to St. Anne, according to the calendar of the Byzantine Rite. These hymns and collects came to me through the thoughtful kindness of a devout Greek friend, Velissarios Feeris, himself a writer of note; and, in the belief that other English and American readers may be as unfamiliar with them as I was, I am presenting them herewith, exactly as they were presented to me:

Feast of the Forefathers of God—Joachim and Anna. September 9th.

Dismissal Hymn. We celebrate, O Lord, the memory of Thy just and blessed forefathers, and through them we implore Thee: Save our souls.

Collect. Now Anna rejoices that she is set free from the bonds of her barrenness, and she nourishes the most holy Child. She calls together all people to praise Him, Who from her womb gave to mortals the only Virgin Mother.

Feast of the Conception of St. Anna, the Mother of the Virgin. December 9th.

Dismissal Hymn. Today the bonds of barrenness are loosed; for God heard the prayer of Joachim and Anna, and contrary to hope promised to them clearly that they should bear a divine Maiden; for from her He, the Infinite, was born, Who became mortal and Who commanded to the Angel, to announce to her: Hail, thou that art full of grace, the Lord is with thee.

Collect. The world commemorates today the conception, by the grace of God, of Anna; for she conceived the conception of the Word which is beyond word.

Feast of the Repose of St. Anne, Mother of the Virgin. July 25th.

Dismissal Hymn. Thou, O holy Anne, didst bear the bearer of Life, the pure mother of God. Wherefore now that by Heaven's decree, rejoicing in glory, thou hast gone over to where the blessed dwell, do thou entreat mercy for transgressions unto those who with desire honor thee, O blessed Saint.

Collect. Let us celebrate the memory of the ancestors of Christ, and faithfully entreat their help, that all may be delivered from all tribulation, who cry: God be with us, Who glorifieth according to His good pleasure.

PART III.

Songs of St. Anne

Statue of St. Anne holding the Virgin and the Virgin holding the Christ Child. Cathedral, Avila. (This triple treatment is very characteristic of medieval Spanish statues.)

Songs of St. Anne

The canticles, hymns, songs and poems connected with St. Anne have almost as early an origin as her cult and are now almost as numerous as her shrines. The first of these were naturally written in Latin and Greek, and these are the languages in which they are still presented for liturgical use in Churches of Greek and Roman rites. However, they quickly crept into the vernacular, and now exist not only in most national languages, but in many of more local usage, like Breton and Provençal, for instance. Some offer petitions to St. Anne or sing her praises; others tell her story, in more or less complete form, and lay considerable stress on her role as a grandmother. Most are reverent, almost worshipful in character; but a few are rollicking folk songs. Besides those devoted entirely to her, she appears incidentally in many which treat several other subjects; and there is a medieval mystery play in which she figures as a leading character.

The earliest surviving hymn in her honor appears to be one written in Greek during the fifth century by St. Romanus. Two centuries later, Andrew of Damascus, Archbishop of Crete, wrote a whole series of hymns praising her, in the same language. His contemporary, St. Sophrone, Archbishop of Jerusalem, wrote in the same vein, though more briefly, in Latin. From then on, the songs of St. Anne increased rapidly in quantity and variety. Erasmus and Chaucer were only two among the great medieval poets who lauded her. In the nineteenth century Thomas Moore, during the course of a trip down the St. Lawrence River, wrote the words for an air which was the constant refrain of Canadian boatmen, and left an interesting account of the circumstances under which he did so. The number of songs and poems more recently addressed to St. Anne or describing her are legion.

To anyone needing or wishing to make a thorough survey of all these canticles, hymns, songs and poems, and their correlative liturgical invocations, I cannot too highly commend the section devoted to these in *Les Trois Légendes de Madame Saincte Anne,* the comprehensive and authoritative work of P. V. Charland, to which I have referred and from which I have quoted, so often before. The following selection includes only poems and songs written *in English,* which are in the minority; it was almost entirely culled from this invaluable source and is gratefully presented herewith through kind permission.

I have said, quite accurately, that most of the poems included in this volume are culled from Father Charland's comprehensive collection. Among the exceptions are one taken from *The Sponsor,* a pamphlet issued by The Servants of the Paraclete at Jemez Springs, New Mexico; one taken from *St. Anne of Talavila* which, according to the author, The Rt. Rev. Dr. Edmund Peiris, was found in a palm leaf manuscript, dated March 21, 1806, which is a Tamil Hymn, freely anglicized; and my own sonnet to Ste. Anne de Beaupré, which has been previously published in *The Happy Wanderer* and is included here at the request of the Editors.

Tamil Hymn to St. Anne of Palakkuda

Mid copses and forests, where drums and cymbals sound—
With a lagoon on one side, where fish frolick and sport,
On the other, the wide expanse of rock-fringed ocean—
Mid *palu* trees with berries, luscious and shedding nectar,
Stands the great sanctuary of far-famed Palakkuda,
Where mercy is poured in torrents unending,
Where the sick are cured and restored to health,
Where favours full many and miracles so countless
Are wrought by St. Anne, who gave to this earth
A daughter all sublime, Mary, the stainless:
I worship her feet, at her shrine venerated.

Oh Thou That Art so Fair

And for that faith is dead withouten workis,
So for to worken give me wit and grace!
That I be quit from thence that most dark is.
O thou that art so fair and full of grace,
Be thou mine advocate in that high place,
There, as withouten end is sung Hozanne,
Thou Christes mother, daughter dear of Anne!

—Geoffrey Chaucer.

Carol of Joy

Joy comes at length to all hearts that believed,
And the sighs of the saints must at last end in song:
The best gifts of God fall to those who have grieved,
And his love is the stronger for waiting so long.

Oh blest be the day when old earth bore its fruit,
The fairest of daughters it ever had seen,
In the village that lies at the white mountain-foot,
And the angels sang song to the young Nazarene!

Mid the carols of shepherds, the bleating of sheep,
The joy of that birth, blessed Anne, came to thee,
When the fruits were grown golden, the grapes blushing deep,
In the fields and the orchards of green Galilee.

O Anne! joyous saint! what a life didst thou live!
What an unbroken brightness of innocent bliss!
Ev'ry touch of thy child a fresh rapture could give . . .
Yet didst thou not kneel ere thou daredst to kiss?

—Père Faber.

Saint Anne

Hail pious mother, holy Anna hail!
Thy name falls sweetly on the Christian's ear;
They called thee *gracious*, chosen to prevail
By grace, throughout thy heav'nward journey here.

Root of yon Branch, whose heav'nly blossoms sent
Wide o'er the earth the perfume of its breath;
Perennial fount, e'er spreading, never spent,
Lily of Jesse, Rose of Nazareth.

Hail mother of that Star which placid rose
Above the flood of death and sin and war;
The mother of our Queen whom Heaven chose
Spouse of the King of kings for evermore!

Receive our supplications, mother dear,
Who merited alone, of all mankind,
The honor to conceive, to nurse and rear
God's stainless Mother, for our joy designed.

Oh, never cease, we pray thee, to present
Before that Son and Mother our desire,
The King and Queen of yonder firmament,
That happy home to which our souls aspire.

—Père Faber.

A Canadian Boat Song

Faintly as tolls the evening chime,
Our voices keep tune and our oars keep time.
Soon as the woods on shore look dim,
We'll sing at St. Ann's our parting hymn.
Row, brothers, row, the stream runs fast,
The Rapids are near, and the daylight's past!

Why should we yet our sail unfurl?
There is not a breath the blue wave to curl!
But when the wind blows off the shore,
Oh! sweetly we'll rest our weary oar.
Blow, breezes, blow, the stream runs fast,
The Rapids are near, and the daylight's past!

Ottawa tide! this trembling moon
Shall see us float over thy surges soon.
Saint of this green Isle! hear our prayers,
Oh! grant us cool heavens and favouring airs!
Blow, breezes, blow, the stream runs fast,
The Rapids are near, and the daylight's past!

The following notation appears with the poem in the *Complete Poetical Works of Thomas Moore*, published in Paris, in 1827.

"I wrote these words to an air which our boatmen sung to us very frequently. The wind was so unfavourable that they were obliged to row all the way, and we were five days in descending the river from Kingston to Montreal, exposed to an intense sun during the day, and at night forced to take shelter from the dews in any miserable hut upon the banks that would receive us. But the magnificent scenery of the St. Lawrence repays all such difficulties. Our *Voyageurs* had good voices, and sung perfectly in tune together. The original words of the air to which I adapted these stanzas, appeared to be a long incoherent story, of which I could understand but little, from the barbarous pronounciation of the Canadians."

Hymn to Saint Anne

Spotless Anna! Juda's glory!
Through the Church, from East to West,
Ev'ry tongue proclaims thy praises,
Holy Mary's Mother blest.

Saintly kings and priestly sires
Blended in thy sacred line;
Thou in virtue, all before thee
Didst excell by grace divine.

Linked in bonds of purest wedlock,
Thine it was for us to bear,
By the favor of high Heaven,
Our eternal Virgin Star.

From thy stem in beauty budded
Ancient Jesse's mystic rod;
Earth from thee received the Mother
Of th'almighty Son of God.

All the human race benighted
In the depths of darkness lay,
When in Anne it saw the dawning
Of the long expected day.

Honor, glory, virtue, merit,
Be to Thee, O Virgin's Son!
With the Father and the Spirit,
While eternal ages run.

—EDWARD CASWALL,
from *The Dominican Hymn book,* published by
Burns and Oates, London, 1881.

St. Anne Speaks to Her Daughter Mary:

"Child of my heart's blood,
Fairest Lily of all Israel,
Embraced by the Most High,
Rapturously pillowed on His Love,
Clothed in Glory from the first
Sacred Instant of your conception by the Power
Of the Spirit of Charity! Mary, My Child!
Whence is it to me that the Mother of My
Lord should come unto me." Thus Anne spoke and
Joachim kept all these things pondering them
In his heart. The days had been so long but at last
Heaven had listened and answered with Mary.

Mary Speaks to Her Mother Anne:

"A daughter radiates goodness from God through her mother.
The royal blood coursing through my heart I took from you and
Gave it to Him, Who loved all He had chosen even unto the
Death of the cross—a tree which would shudder and be honored by
The last tear of His Precious Blood.
Know, Mother Anne, that on the night wherein He was betrayed
Solemnly He spoke, searching the heart of each disciple
And loving all who through them should love Him,
This is the Chalice of My Blood which shall be shed
For many unto the remission of sins.
My Son's Holy Cup He made a ruddy link forged in
Majestic Fire to weld all souls to Him—

Flaming red His Precious Blood from the Font of our
Hearts, O Anna, rushed in torrents like
Golden sunlight into the hearts of those who believe that
He is the Way, the Truth and the Light.
Courageously It mingled with the Blood of
Stephen and Peter and Agnes and Isaac Jogues and
Father Pro—Quietly It gave health and strength to
Little children as they watched the
Heavens open and the Lord Jesus of brightest Hope
Smile a welcome—even as many centuries from then sainted
Thomas More would graciously find another scaffold and
Smile as his life's blood unites with the
Blood of love."

—The Sponsor

The Feast of St. Anne

In swarms of arrowy canoes they came—
Flotillas dancing o'er the wide Bras-d'Or,
And bark more ponderous, with sail and oar,
Equipped and managed with the white man's skill—
From many an Indian Village near and far,
The favoured of their frequent shifting homes . . .

From Malagwatchkit's mazy shores they came;
From where Benacadie and Eskasoni
Are linked by hill and shore to deep Tweedmooge;
From Wagamatkook's stream of golden sands,
Whykokomagh, sweet nestling midst its hills—
And Boularderie, and mountain-girt St. Anne's—
And where, beneath Victoria mountains lone
Looks Ingonishe upon the ocean main;
And many other dell, and stream and shore,
To those dark natives of the soil most dear,
In this last stronghold of their fading race.

There come the old and young of either sex
From tottering dotard to the new-born babe—
All bent to keep the feast of Good Saint Anne,
And still grave council hold, as in the past,
When deeds momentous waited on their words.

—From the *Cosmopolitan Review.*

To Saint Anne

Garden of God, whose mystic Rose
On thy pure breast found her repose,
Hiding within her heart of gold
Balsams of mercies manifold,
Destined to soothe, to heal, to bless,
Earth in her dreariest hours' distress.

Garden of God, whose Lily-flower,
Was thy most precious crown and dower,
Fair snowy perianth of threes,
Outer and inner trinities,
Types of the Triune God above,
And Nazareth's Trinity of Love.

Garden of God! O great St. Anne!
Gladden our lifetime's narrow span
With thy pure Flower of peace and love,
That in God's Paradise above
Opens her snowy blooms and grace
In the full sunshine of God's Face.

—Louise Morison

The Mother of the Madonna

There is one sweet Saint above
Whom I fear we do not love
With the love which is her meed.
Worthy of our love indeed
Is the good and kind St. Anne:
Let us praise her all we can.

She within whose virgin breast
Babe Divine took sweetest rest,
Jesus' Mother meek and mild,
Nay, she *is* thy child on high—
Where she reigns, thou must be nigh.

Thine, O Mother! the delight
To behold this blossom bright
Opening out in beauty rare;
Thine to hear her infant prayer;
Thine with wondering love to trace
Her increase in peerless grace.

Hadst thou gone from earth before
Gabriel to Mary bore
Marvellous message from above?
Did thy tender Daughter's love
Hover o'er thy parting breath,
Sweetening the pang of death?

This we know not—but we know
That in heaven, as here below,
Blessed Mary, meek and mild,
Is thy grateful, loving child.
Oh! how great thy power must be!
Use it, kind St. Anne, for me.

Bid thy Daughter ask her Son
To forgive the wrongs I've done,
And, in spite of all to spare.
She will heed her mother's prayer—
And *His* Mother's prayer, 'tis plain,
Never, never can be vain.

What new grace shall I implore?
Ah! to feel yet more and more
Of that filial love and zeal
Which the Breton peasants feel—
Honoring as best I can
Mary's Mother, good St. Anne.

—Matthew Russell, S.J.

The Bells of Saint-Anne

Now from their turret gray and old,
Where call the swallows in the gloom,
The tender bells of eventide
Float out across the night's perfume;
The music from their throbbing throats
Stirs the shadows like a flame,
And all the drowsing world grows glad
With love for holy one they name:
"Sainte Anne!" their mellow voices cry:
"Sainte Anne!" "La bonne sainte Anne!"
"Sainte Anne!"

The far dim stretch of meadow grass
Is all a-glimmer with the dew;
Its shining drops fall soft as tears
When slips the evening zephyr through.
From out some mesh of soft brown blades,
A last, late thrush pipes low and sweet;
And once again the faithful bells
Their sacred melody repeat:
"Sainte Anne!" they murmur in reply:
"Sainte Anne!" "La bonne sainte Anne!"
"Sainte Anne!"

Along the river's winding length
The tide is running fleet and white;
It drowns the reeds along the shore,
And hides the sandy bar from sight;
Vague sadness freights the misty air;
Night settles like a thing of woe;
And in their watch-tower high and still
The bells are swaying soft and slow:
"Saint Anne!"—the faint notes break and die:
"Sainte Anne!" "La bonne sainte Anne!"
"Sainte Anne!". . .

Anonymous.

· 170 ·

Prayer of Guidance

White star above the Ocean,
Guide thou, St. Ann, our bark:
Lead us in pure devotion
Safe thro' the tempest dark.

St. Ann, in Heaven shining,
There in thy glorious home,
T'ward thee our hearts inclining,
Bless us where'er we roam!

To wounded soldiers lying
Lone on the battle field,
And sailors storm defying,
Thy help and comfort yield!

St. Ann, in Heaven shining,
There in thy glorious home,
T'ward thee our hearts inclining,
Bless us where'er we roam!

Sweet Mother, with thy healing,
Thou dost the lame restore;
The blind before Thee kneeling
Behold Heaven's light once more!

St. Ann, in Heaven shining,
There in thy glorious home,
T'ward thee our hearts inclining,
Bless us where'er we roam!

Cure then our fervor halting;
To our blind hearts give sight;
To Mary's love exalting,
Bring us to Jesus' light.

—From the magazine *The Child,*
November 1894.

Sung to the air: *Home, Sweet Home.*

Ste. Anne de Beaupré

Ste. Anne de Beaupré—sheltered by the snow,
Within a gray church, under skies of gray,
It seems to me that I can hear you say
In vibrant accents, gentle, soft and low—
"Kneel at my lighted shrine before you go
Back to the careless world so hard and gay—
It matters not if you have gone astray,
I will deliver you from pain and woe—
If you are bowed with grief and suffering,
If you are sore at heart, or stained with sin,
Why should you feel this is a hopeless thing?
I still can heal and cleanse—Come in, Come in."

And my soul answers, "Oh, I know you can,
For I have felt your miracle, Ste. Anne!"

Frances Parkinson Keyes
from *The Happy Wanderer*

Uffizi Gallery, Florence

The Virgin with Her Son and St. Anne. Mosaccio.

APPENDIX

References, Bibliography, Author's Note

References

INTRODUCTION

1. I am indebted to the Rev. John Reynolds of the Archconfraternity of St. Ann in New Orleans for the suggestion which prompted this paragraph.

2. This experience is fully related in the author's book, *Along a Little Way*.

3. I have found a record of no less than 221 chapels dedicated to St. Anne in Brittany.

4. I found a notable exception to this general rule in a sermon preached on St. Anne's Day at Lac St. Joseph, Quebec, by the Rev. Bernard Morisset, Professor of Theology at Laval University. I am quoting elsewhere from this splendid sermon, in which the central theme is St. Anne's role as a grandmother.

Part I

5. Some early authorities, among them St. James the Less, give the name of Anne's father as Akar and do not mention her mother's name at all; among the most eminent writers of modern times to do the same is probably the French writer, Émile Rey, whose superb biography, entitled *L'Aieule du Christ: Sainte Anne de Jérusalem*, has been crowned by the French Academy and officially approved by the Vatican. The Reverend P. A. Laïly of the French White Fathers, who have long been custodians of the Church of St. Anne in Jerusalem, traditionally the site of the home of Anne and Joachim, accepts Rey's version and approves the genealogy given in his book, which is herewith reproduced:

AKAR

déscendant d'Aaron.

ISMERIE	ANNE
née en 63 avant J.-C.	née en 55 avant J.-C.
épouse un sacrificateur	épouse *Joachim*
(de sa tribu)	(de la tribu de Juda)
ELISABETH	MARIE
née en 45 avant J.-C.	née en 16 avant J.-C.
épouse *Zacharie*	(la *Vierge-Mère*)
Saint JEAN-BAPTISTE	JESUS
né en l'an I	né en l'an I

Other eminent modern writers, among them Eugene Lefebvre and Roger Baudier, give the name of Anne's father as Stollan and that of her mother as Emerentiana, and quote various early Fathers of the Church and several medieval and modern writers as their authority, among them St. Cyril of Alexandria, Vincent de Beauvais, Jacques de Voragines—author of *The Golden Legend*—and Canon Athanase Olliver, the late pastor of Ste. Anne's at Nantes, whom I had also hoped to consult personally, only to find that he had recently died. Baudier further says, "Stollan was a young man of the wealthy class, descendant of a royal family, who bore an excellent reputation among the people of Israel who live north of Carmel. He was a man of virtue, who followed the Law and served the Lord in the fullness of his youth."

The Rev. Paul-Victor Charland, O.P., in his masterly work, *Les Trois Légendes de Madame Saincte Anne,* devotes a whole chapter to this controversial subject without committing himself on either side. I have purposely avoided discussing the names of Anne's parents in the narrative proper, as this seemed to me only to add an element of confusion to a story which I was trying to make primarily vivid and lucid, and also, to make it seem less real to the average lay reader, while adding very little to its essential authenticity, since both versions of the story agree in making Anne's father fitted for and worthy of service in the temple. For purposes of complete documentation, however, of course the conflicting opinions and the reasons for them should be given.

6. Roger Baudier.

7. The following description is an abbreviated adaptation—not a literal translation—of the last part of Chapter II in Émile Rey's *L'Aïeule du Christ: Saint Anne de Jérusalem.*

8. See Luke III, Verses 23 and 24: "And Jesus himself was beginning about the age of thirty years: being (as it was supposed) the son of Joseph, *who was the son of Heli,* who was of Mathat," [or Mathas] The names Heliakim, Eliakim and Joachim are all synonymous in Hebrew. Reference is made to the male line as was then customary, since Joseph was married to Mary; but Joseph was actually, of course, the *son-in-law* of Joachim, not the son. In the Jewish Talmud also, Mary is described as the daughter of Heliakim or Joachim. According to St. Matthew, the name of Joseph's own father was Jacob. (See Matthew I, Verse 16.)

9. Numbers XXXVI. 6-10.

10. Esther IX.

11. Genesis XLIX. 10.

12. *Les Trois Légendes de Madame Saincte Anne* by Rev. Paul-Victor Charland.

13. The source material on which these two last assertions are based will be found quoted in the next chapter.

14. Charland, p. 155, quoting from a letter written by Lavigerie to the Bishop of Vannes.

15. Although such references are lacking, it is interesting to note that Pope Pius X changed the date of his feast day from March 20th to August 16th, obviously so that it might be observed in connection with the Feast of the Assumption of the Blessed Virgin on August 15th, thus associating father and daughter in the minds of the devout.

16. Luke, Chapter II. Verses 41-52.

17. Leviticus. Chapter XXV. Verse 10.

18. I have felt justified in discounting completely the legend of the Trinubium; and, since there is good authority (see p. 71 of text) for believing that Joachim lived until shortly after the birth of Jesus, I have, throughout this part of the story, decided against risking further confusion to the reader by giving two versions of it. This decision was taken only when I found that none of its essentials would have been changed if Anne had become a widow somewhat earlier.

19. It should be borne in mind that at this time there was no secular law, as there is now in many places, forbidding the marriage of first cousins; on the contrary, such marriages were encouraged, not only among the Jews, but among many other peoples. Canon law, of course, did not exist until much later.

20. Luke I. Verses 26-38.

21. Isaias VII. Verse 14.

22. I feel that thoughtful persons, whatever their form of faith, owe a great debt of gratitude to the Jewish writer, Scholem Asch, for clarifying this legal point in his novel entitled *Mary*. For centuries, it has been so universal to think of Mary as the Holy Mother, we are apt to forget that, in the little town where she lived, she might well have been the subject of cruel and mendacious gossip, if her family and her future husband had not stood by her. While Asch's book does not, of course, conform to the tenets of Catholicism—nor could it—it is written with great reverence and with meticulous care on such points as these.

23.   To me there is a very pleasant link between the legend of St. Anne's laurel tree, in Jerusalem, with which she is frequently shown in medieval paintings, and the laurels which surround the church embellished by the ninth century mosaics which tell the story of her life, and which also show her with her laurel tree, at Daphni—the Greek word for laurel—near Athens.

24.   The best description I have found of this feeling and this custom is in Christina Hole's fine book, *English Shrines and Sanctuaries,* and reads as follows:

"Many of the great mediaeval shrines drew their sanctity simply from the presence of relics which had been brought in from outside and were not necessarily connected with any local tradition. The cult of relics came to its full height during the Middle Ages, but *it was already ancient when that period began.* In every age, including our own, the remains of the great have been venerated because, instinctively, mankind has always felt that holiness is not affected by the mere accident of death. From very early times traces of a man's essential virtue have been thought to cling about his mortal leavings, even though his spirit has passed to another and better world. Nowadays we are not always conscious that our respect springs from this underlying belief, but in fact it is so; and it is one of the differences between ourselves and the mediaeval Christian that he was fully aware of it and followed his belief to its logical conclusion.

"The bones and blood of the saints, their garments, and whatever they had touched or used in life, were for him imbued with spiritual force, as those of the pagan heroes had been for his predecessors. He expected miracles from them as naturally as he expected flowers in summer and storms in winter. With deep and true devotion he encased them in lovely jewelled shrines, housed them in buildings which are still the glory of our land, and travelled over long distances to pray and make his vows before them. No earthly treasure of gold or silver compared in its owner's estimation with these reminders of the holy dead, and every source of artistry, craftsmanship, and money was generously expended upon the caskets and shrines in which they were preserved.

"This very real reverence had its worldly side also, which sometimes resulted in rather peculiar happenings. Miracle-working relics were a source of considerable wealth as well as glory to their guardians, and every monastery and parish was ambitious to possess them. Since the supply was naturally limited, this often led to unfortunate rivalries, and to the ransacking of graves which should have been protected by the very feeling that caused them to be despoiled. Few of the saints were allowed to rest in peace. They were dug up, quarrelled over, translated from one church to another, and ruthlessly dismembered. Their bones were divided between numerous shrines, and the smallest object connected with them was ardently coveted, fetched from afar, presented by generous donors as the finest gift in their power to bestow, bought at a great price, and sometimes even stolen."

25. Acts II, Verses 4-11. Acts IV, 4. Acts V, 14.

26. Although it is asserted on good authority that these relics had wrapped about them the type of winding sheet used for the burial of the dead at this period, it should be carefully noted that no claim has ever been made to the effect that *all* of St. Anne's mortal remains were removed, thus early in the Christian Era, from the sepulchre at Nazareth. The so-called Aptian Legend, which this author is herewith presenting, in no way nullifies the claims of Constantinople, and hence of Chartres, to an authentic relic, the former claim dating from the 4th Century.

27. The center where they worked is still known by their names, or rather by that of Mary Magdalene, as well as of Mary Salome and Mary Jacobe, for she is also traditionally buried there. It is called *Les Trois Maries,* and is especially famous for the biennial pilgrimage of Gipsies, who regard Mary Magdalene as their patron saint, and who foregather there in large numbers.

28. To this statement, Rey adds the following footnote: "After having made careful inquiries regarding the St. Anne relics, Charlemagne would have instigated a search at Nazareth, if he had not had reason to believe that these would be found at Apt. He did not make any at the former place, but at the latter. When he was convinced that the mortal remains of Christ's grandmother were indeed at Apt, he took the measures which led to their rediscovery. This is why, from that time on, the church there was one of those most dear to the heart of the Emperor."

29. Rey does not mention the fact that Charlemagne's coronation robes were embroidered with a figure of St. Anne, but this was stressed in the sermon delivered by the Bishop of Vannes at Ste. Anne d'Auray on the Saint's Feast Day, July 26, 1955.

30. *Les Trois Légendes de Madame Saincte Anne* by Paul-Victor Charland, p. 208.

31. According to Father Ronan, "The winding sheet in which the body of St. Anne was wrapped is very ancient and of Oriental texture. It is of very fine cotton, with a gold embroidery all around the edges, and with a line of unknown characters forming another band all around. The same embroidery runs up the center of the sheet and then dividing is joined to three groups of other characters traced in three oval cartouches between which are represented two monsters of human form, back to back, having ancient crowns on their head and with extended wings. Under their feet and above their crowns are ovals to hold some kind of ointment. The length of the sheet is nine feet four inches, and its breadth four feet eight inches. The figures and the characters have doubtless some unknown mysterious significance.

"Joseph Suarez, Bishop of Vaison, already referred to, having carefully examined the material and texture of the winding sheet, is of opinion that it was made in Egypt and that the body it enclosed came from the Holy Land."

32. Probably the most famous of all these was Anne of Austria, Queen Consort of Louis XIII. Dubreil gives us a moving account of the situation which led to this pilgrimage and also, of its results: "The direct posterity of Henri IV was on the point of becoming extinct. The king had no heir to carry it on, to be the personification of the greatness that was everywhere evident. In the gloomy melancholy that he felt, Louis saw a ray of hope, or rather he saw it in his spouse. Her name was Anne, and something told her that she did not bear that name in vain. She turned her eyes toward Apt and, full of confidence, she sent a large and brilliant deputation to register a vow, that of the whole nation, at the feet of St. Anne.

"Never was prayer so solemn, and never was prayer more generously heard. The Queen, a long time barren, became a mother in spite of her advanced age, and gave a son to the race of Henri IV, to her royal spouse, and this son was Louis XIV, the great king, who was famous in French history . . . .

"The mother of Louis XIV [Anne of Austria] left Paris to show her gratitude at Apt. Charlemagne had not been unmindful, neither will she. Charlemagne had built, over the crypt and over the temple built by S. Castor, one of his forty churches; Anne [of Austria], in order to perpetuate the memory of her visit and of the protection of which she had been the object, had a side chapel built to the cathedral, on the plan of S. Mary Major's [in Rome], to which the body of S. Anne, with the other relics associated with it, have since been transferred.

"These two edifices [the side-chapel and the cathedral], stoutly built to last through the centuries, will go down to posterity as a memorial of what France has been for the Grandmother of Christ, and of what the Grandmother of Christ has been for France. They will say to all generations who come to reverence at her shrine that the greatest of emperors and the greatest of kings have been blessed by her, that their reigns have been inaugurated under her eyes; they will say that the two most beautiful pages of our French history, as well as those of some saints, and of many others, have been begun at the foot of her altar."

33. S. Anne Her Cult and Her Shrines, Rev. Myles V. Ronan, C.C., M.R.I.A., p. 28.

34. *Mary Magdalene* by Père La Cordaire.

Part II

35. *English Shrines and Sanctuaries, Christian Hole*, p. 10.

36. Thomas Cromwell, Earl of Essex (1485-1540), the Vicar General of Henry VIII, is frequently confused with General Oliver Cromwell, the Puritan statesman and Lord Protector of the Commonwealth (1599-1658). In justice to the latter, who unquestionably is answerable for many other acts of desecration, let it be said that he was not responsible for the first of these which took place in England during the Reformation.

37. *English Shrines and Sanctuaries*, Christina Hole, pp. 145 and 162.

38. Much of the development of Buxton is due to the Dukes of Devonshire. The bath building, which was substituted for the one erected by the Earl of Shrewsbury, was built by the third Earl of Devonshire in 1670 and the impetus for the famous Crescent came from one of his successors. The present Duke has served as Mayor of Buxton.

39. Rev. Eugene Lefebvre.

40. The Reverend Eugene Lefebvre, C.S.S.R., is the author of several books and pamphlets of great value, among them: *La Morale Anice de l'Art: Profils d'Apôtres: Terri de Miracles: La Bonne Sainte Anne: Life of Saint Anne: A Novena to Saint Anne: Saint Anne's Prayer Book.*

41. How far this Apostolate has now spread may be judged from the fact that even in such remote regions of Louisiana as Cow Island there is a church dedicated to St. Anne, whose pastor, the Rev. Marcel Murie, broadcasts regularly in French and has been particularly effective in combating anti-Catholic propaganda.

42. There are, in Japan, at least two other parishes under the patronage of St. Anne: Koryama, in the Diocese of Sendai; and Muroran, in the Apostolic Vicarate of Sapporo. They were founded respectively in 1887 and 1893 by the *Pères des Missions Étrangeres de Paris;* each group contains about 200 Catholics in the midst of a population of about 100,000. The feast of the patroness is solemnly celebrated. At Muroran, it is the day dedicated for the First Holy Communion. St. Anne is invoked after every public prayer and after Mass. .

Bibliography

THE HOLY BIBLE—Douay Version

LA SAINTE BIBLE Éditions de Maredsous—Éditions Zech et fils Baine-le-Comte.

APOCHRYPHAL NEW TESTAMENT translated by M. R. James. Published in Oxford at the Clarendon Press, 1924.

THE LOST BOOKS OF THE BIBLE translated from the original tongues. (The names of the translator or translators is not given on the title page)

GOSPEL OF PSEUDO-MATTHEW

THE GOLDEN LEGEND by Jacques de Voragines.

L'AÏEULE DU CHRIST SAINTE ANNE DE JÉRUSALEM by Émile Rey, Laureat de l'Academie Francaise.

THE LIFE OF ST. ANN by Roger Baudier. Published in St. Ann's Herald by the Archconfraternity of St. Ann, New Orleans (January, 1928-June, 1929).

LES TROIS LÉGENDES DE MADAME SAINCTE ANNE by Père Paul-Victor Charland. Published by Wm. Charland & Co., Montreal.

LE CULTE DE SAINTE ANNE EN OCCIDENT by Père Paul-Victor Charland. Published by Franciscaine Missionnaire, Quebec.

SAINTE MARIE OÙ ELLE EST NÉE ET LA PISCINE PROBATIQUE by N. Van der Vliet of the Pères Blancs. Published by J. Gabalda, Paris.

DIE HEILIGE ANNA: IHRE VEREHRUNG IN GESCHICHTE, KUNST, UND VOLKS-TUM by von Beda Kleinschmidt. Published by L. Schwann, Düsseldorff.

SAINTE-ANNE DE JÉRUSALEM by Mgr. Philippe Gorra. Published by Saint Paul, Harissa-Liban.

LES GUIDES BLEUS—Provence and Bretagne. Published by Librairie Hachette, Paris.

CHARLEMAGNE FROM THE HAMMER TO THE CROSS by Richard Winston. Published by The Bobbs-Merrill Company, Inc.

S. ANNE HER CULT AND HER SHRINES by Rev. Myles V. Ronan, C.C., M.R.I.A. Published by Sands & Co., London.

ENGLISH SHRINES AND SANCTUARIES by Christina Hole. Published by B. T. Batsford Ltd.

IN SARA'S TENTS by Walter Starkie. Published by E. P. Dutton & Co., Inc.

ST. ANNE OF TALAVILA by The Rt. Rev. Dr. Edmund Peiris, O.M.I., Bishop of Chilaw.

LIFE OF SAINT ANNE by Rev. Eugene Lefebvre, C.Ss.R. Published at Ste. Anne de Beaupré.

THE SPONSOR. Published by The Servants of the Paraclete, Jemez Springs, New Mexico.

LEGENDS OF THE MADONNA by Anna Jameson. Published by Houghton Mifflin Co.

Author's Note

The author's travels, undertaken in connection with writing this book, include the localities most closely connected with St. Anne's life and present cult, namely, Palestine, Provence, Brittany and Quebec; also, that portion of Old England—Derbyshire—where her cult former-ly flourished and of which there are the most arresting modern sequels, and that portion of New England—northwestern Vermont—which has the most interesting historical association with her veneration in the United States.

New Orleans, which, for the past ten years, has been the author's writing center during the winter, has provided, without the necessity for special travel, both the data for the historical associations with the cult of St. Anne in Louisiana, and the shrine at which this cult is so fully and faithfully observed today.

In all these places, the author has met with the greatest kindness and co-operation in the pursuit of her work. It would be literally impossi-ble to mention all the persons who have helped her, but among them the following are outstanding: Their Royal Highnesses, the Infante Don Alfonso and the Infanta Dona Beatriz of Orleans; The Reverend Ana Maria Gomez, Abbess of the Convent of Santa Ana, Avila, Spain; The Reverend Eugene Lefebvre, Director of Pilgrimages at Ste. Anne de Beaupré, and one of the greatest living authorities on St. Anne; The Reverend I. Gammond, Curé of St. Anne's Cathedral at Apt; The Reverend Monsignor J. Corniquel, Director of Pilgrimages at Ste. Anne d'Auray; The Reverend John Reynolds, Assistant Director of the Arch-confraternity of St. Ann's in New Orleans, and Mr. Roger Baudier, the well-known author, also of New Orleans, who, like Father Lefebvre, has devoted years of study to the subject of St. Anne and who is active in the work of the Archconfraternity; The Reverend P. Laïly of the White Fathers in charge of St. Anne's of Jerusalem; The Reverend Mother Aloysius of the College of the Blessed Virgin Mary in Seville; Mrs. Pelham Cochrane of Vence; The Reverend J. J. Fitzgerald of St. Edmund's Seminary, Burlington, Vermont; The Prioress and several of the nuns at the Abbaye des Benedictines, Lisieux; Sister Claire of the Presentation Convent in Buxton, Derbyshire; Mr. R. A. Lockwood, Honorary General Secretary, Wells Dressing Festival, Buxton, Derbyshire; Captain the Hon. John Mitford of Westwell, Burford, Oxford; Mr. David Solomon of the Government Press Information Bureau, Jerusalem; Miss Alison Frantz of the American School of Classical Studies in Athens; Mr. Velissarios Feeris, correspondent in Greece for the NCWC News Service; Miss Katharine McKiever, a member of the Editorial Staff of the NCWC News Service in Washington, D. C.; Miss Mary R. Kennedy of Milton, Vermont; and Mr. Elemore Morgan of Baton Rouge, Louisiana.

Indirect help was also furnished by Miss Muna Lee of the Bureau of Inter-American Affairs, Department of State, Washington, D. C.; Miss Marjorie Canterberry of the American Embassy Staff at Athens and by every member of the Israel Embassy Staff at Washington, from the Ambassador down.

Unquestionably, the greatest debt of all, however, is owed to my secretary, Geraldine Bullock, without whose constant co-operation and unremitting labors, even under the most trying circumstances of frequent illness, rapid travel and correlative handicaps, it would have been impossible for me to meet my deadline. The book was finished while we were in a pitching ship traversing a stormy sea, in a cold, cramped stateroom, so small that in order to dictate from my pencilled draft I had to stay in bed, as there was not room for us both to sit at even the smallest kind of table; and the finished script was airmailed, the last day aboard, from Quarantine because, otherwise, it could not have reached the printer in time to go to press. This is the sort of situation with which a writer is often confronted, but which the reader, who smugly says, "How wonderful to have nothing to do but wait for an inspiration!" never seems to visualize; it is also the sort of situation which reveals the complete lack of understanding on the part of the same reader, who says to the writer's secretary, "How wonderful to go travelling from place to place with a well-known person and have nothing to do but enjoy yourself!" I know all too well how small is the proportion of leisure hours to those spent in hard work for both writer and secretary; to the latter go a full measure of appreciation and heartfelt thanks.

FRANCES PARKINSON KEYES

The text of this book has been set in 12 point Linotype Fairfield, designed by Rudolph Ruzicka.

The display type selected for this book is Monotype Deepdene, designed by Frederic W. Goudy.

Both of these distinguished type faces were selected for their inspirational yet restrained characteristics.

TIZIANO VECELLIO